Harry Potter

ALBUS DUMBLEDORE

Cinematic Guide

SCHOLASTIC LTD.

Copyright © 2016 Warner Bros. Entertainment Inc.
HARRY POTTER characters, names and related
indicia are © & ™ Warner Bros. Entertainment Inc.
WB SHIELD: ™ & © WBEI.
J.K. ROWLING'S WIZARDING WORLD ™
J.K. Rowling and Warner Bros. Entertainment Inc.
Publishing Rights © JKR. (s16)
SCUS37667

www.harrypotter.com

Scholastic Children's Books
Euston House, 24 Eversholt Street,
London NW1 1DB, UK

A division of Scholastic Ltd
London ~ New York ~ Toronto ~ Sydney ~ Auckland
Mexico City ~ New Delhi ~ Hong Kong

First published in the US by Scholastic Inc, 2016
Published in the UK by Scholastic Ltd, 2016

By Felicity Baker
Art Direction: Rick DeMonico
Page Design: Theresa Venezia

ISBN 978 1407 17314 6

Printed and bound by Bell & Bain Ltd, Glasgow

2 4 6 8 10 9 7 5 3 1

All rights reserved

This book is sold subject to the condition that it shall not, by way of trade or otherwise be lent, resold, hired out, or otherwise circulated without the publisher's prior consent in any form or binding other than that in which it is published and without a similar condition, including this condition, being imposed upon the subsequent purchaser.

Papers used by Scholastic Children's Books are made from wood grown in sustainable forests.

www.scholastic.co.uk

Contents

Film Beginnings 4
Life at Hogwarts 14
The Order of the Phoenix 22
Dumbledore and Harry Potter 32
Fighting Dark Forces 40
Legacy 50

Film Beginnings

Albus Dumbledore is one of the most powerful wizards in the world. He studied at Hogwarts School of Witchcraft and Wizardry and went on to become a professor and then Headmaster at Hogwarts.

Albus Percival Wulfric Brian Dumbledore was born in the late nineteenth century. His parents, Percival and Kendra Dumbledore, were both wizards. Albus had a younger brother, Aberforth, and sister, Ariana.

Albus Dumbledore many years before meeting Harry Potter.

Aberforth
Dumbledore

Ariana
Dumbledore

When Albus was young his sister, Ariana, was hurt by some Muggle boys. To protect Ariana, the family moved to Godric's Hollow, a wizarding village.

Godric's Hollow later became home to Harry Potter and his parents, Lily and James.

When Albus was eleven, he went to study at Hogwarts School of Witchcraft and Wizardry.

Like all his fellow students, Albus would call Hogwarts his home while he studied there.

After finishing school, Albus planned to travel the world. But his mother died, so he returned home to care for his brother and sister. There he met Gellert Grindelwald, another young wizard, and the two became fast friends.

Albus Dumbledore (left) with Gellert Grindelwald (right).

The two young men were obsessed with the Deathly Hallows, three all-powerful magical objects said to make the owner master of Death.

The symbol of the Deathly Hallows.

One Deathly Hallow is the Invisibility Cloak.

Another of the three Deathly Hallows is the Resurrection Stone.

The third – and most powerful – Deathly Hallow is the Elder Wand.

Albus's brother, Aberforth, was suspicious of Gellert's greed for power. The three young wizards – Albus, Aberforth and Gellert – duelled, and Ariana was accidentally killed in the fight.

Gellert Grindelwald became one of the most powerful Dark wizards in the world.

After Ariana's death, Albus blamed himself for the tragedy. He mourned Ariana for years.

Albus returned to Hogwarts, where he became a professor.

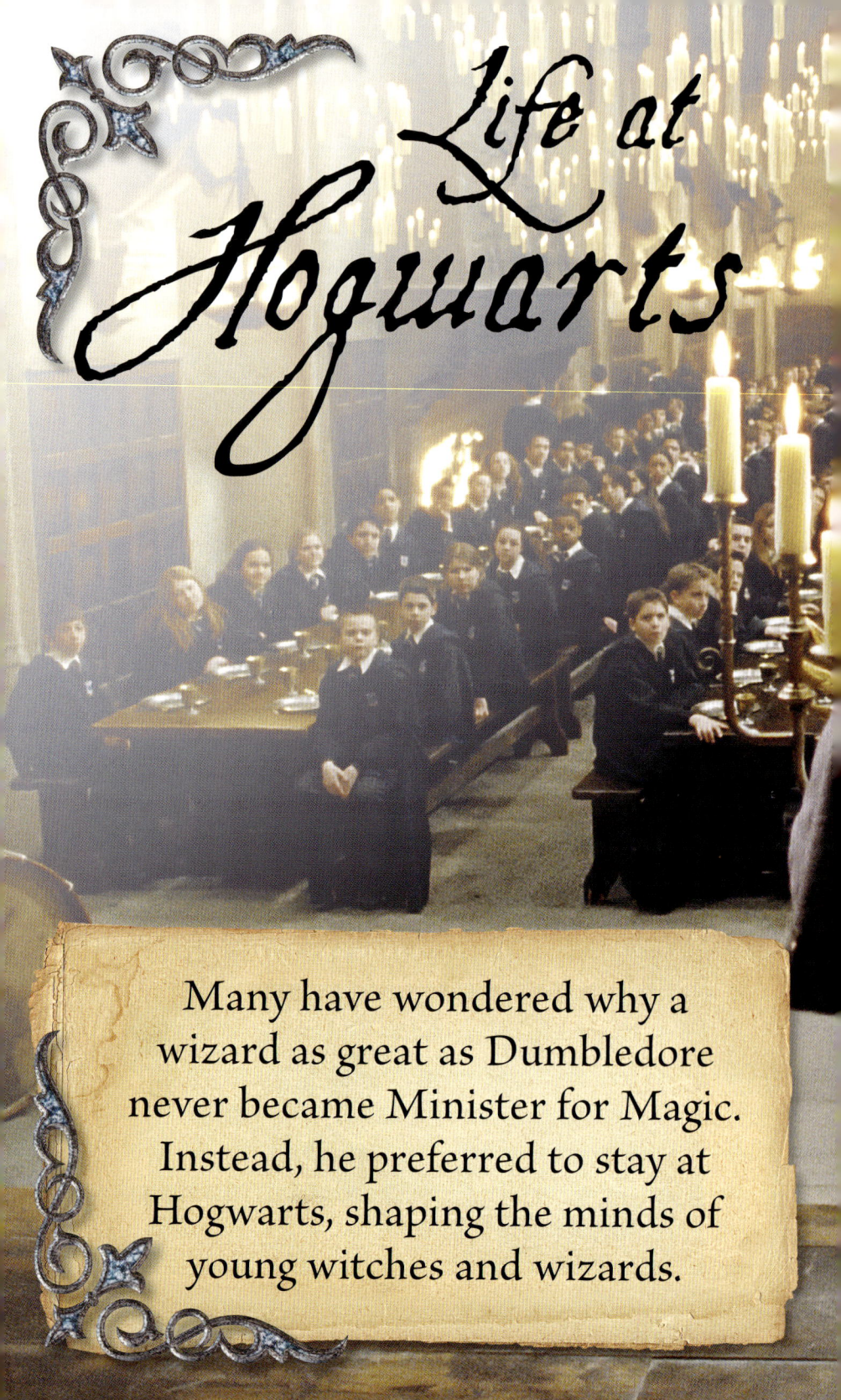

Life at Hogwarts

Many have wondered why a wizard as great as Dumbledore never became Minister for Magic. Instead, he preferred to stay at Hogwarts, shaping the minds of young witches and wizards.

The teachers and students at Hogwarts are devoted to Dumbledore. His closest colleagues at the school include Rubeus Hagrid, Professor McGonagall and Professor Snape.

Minerva McGonagall, Transfiguration professor and Head of Gryffindor house, with Severus Snape, Potions master and Head of Slytherin house.

Rubeus Hagrid, Keeper of the Keys and Grounds.

Dumbledore is so distinguished and well-regarded that young witches and wizards collect Chocolate Frog cards with his picture.

While a professor, Dumbledore brings a troubled young wizard named Tom Riddle to Hogwarts. When Tom gets older, he takes on a new name – Lord Voldemort – and becomes the most powerful Dark wizard the world has ever seen.

Dumbledore meets young Tom Riddle for the first time.

"Did I know that I had just met the most dangerous Dark wizard of all time? No."

— Professor Dumbledore, *Harry Potter and the Half-Blood Prince* film

Dumbledore becomes suspicious of Tom when a student is killed in the Chamber of Secrets. Tom blames Hagrid for the student's death, but Dumbledore is not fooled.

Gellert Grindelwald, the Dark wizard and former friend of Dumbledore, steals the Elder Wand – one of the Deathly Hallows. Dumbledore faces Grindelwald and defeats him, becoming master of the Elder Wand.

Grindelwald steals the Elder Wand from the wandmaker Gregorovitch.

After his duel with Dumbledore, Grindelwald is sent to Nurmengard, a prison in Europe.

There was peace in the wizarding world after Dumbledore defeated Grindelwald, but it did not last long. A new Dark wizard was gaining followers – and this evil lord would prove to be even more dangerous than Grindelwald.

When Lord Voldemort first rises to power, Dumbledore assembles many witches and wizards to fight him. They call themselves the Order of the Phoenix.

A photograph of the original Order of the Phoenix.

> "...the Order of the Phoenix. It's a secret society; Dumbledore founded it..."
>
> – HERMIONE GRANGER, *HARRY POTTER AND THE ORDER OF THE PHOENIX* FILM

The Order's headquarters is hidden at Grimmauld Place.

Dumbledore recruits many of his former students into the Order, including Harry Potter's parents, Lily and James, as well as Sirius Black, Remus Lupin, Alastor "Mad-Eye" Moody, Arthur and Molly Weasley and Minerva McGonagall.

Sirius Black was Lily and James Potter's best friend. The Order uses his childhood home on Grimmauld Place as their headquarters.

Order members Nymphadora Tonks, Molly Weasley, Arthur Weasley and Remus Lupin.

Alastor "Mad-Eye" Moody, Auror for the Ministry of Magic and member of the Order of the Phoenix.

Dumbledore learns of a prophecy about Lord Voldemort and a child who would have the power to defeat the Dark wizard. One of Dumbledore's former students, Severus Snape, overhears the prophecy.

Snape is a Death Eater, and he repeats what he hears of the prophecy to the Dark Lord.

Lord Voldemort is convinced that the prophecy refers to Harry, the child of Lily and James Potter. Harry survives Voldemort's attack, but Lily and James die trying to protect their son.

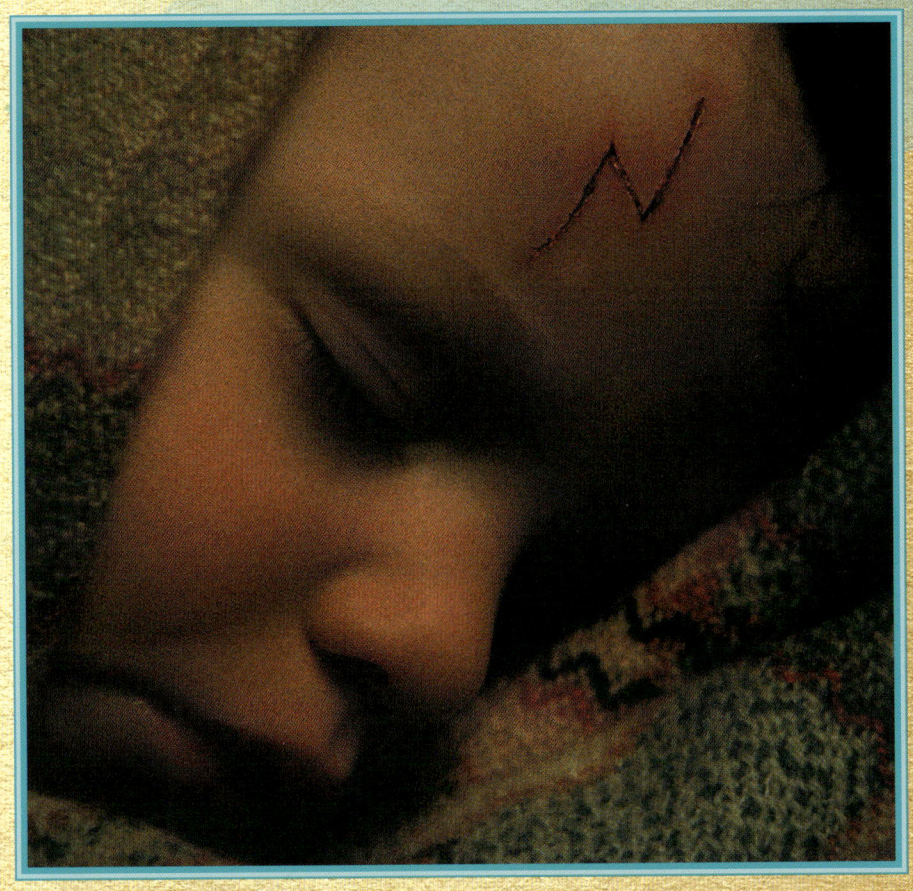

Lily and Snape became friends when they were children at Hogwarts. After Voldemort murders Lily, Snape is devastated. With Dumbledore's help, Snape dedicates his life to protecting Harry.

To avoid suspicion and keep Harry safe, Snape pretends to still be loyal to Voldemort.

Dumbledore and Harry Potter

After Harry's parents die, Dumbledore begins to look out for the boy. Dumbledore comes to care a great deal for Harry. He also knows he must prepare Harry for Voldemort's return.

Professor Dumbledore arranges for baby Harry to live with his relatives, the Dursleys. They are Muggles, the term used by the wizarding community to describe those without magical powers.

Dumbledore and Professor McGonagall bring baby Harry to the Dursleys' home at 4 Privet Drive.

"Good luck, Harry Potter."

– Professor Dumbledore, *Harry Potter and the Philosopher's Stone* film

The summer Harry turns eleven, he receives a letter from Professor McGonagall.

"Dear Mr Potter, we are pleased to inform you that you have been accepted at Hogwarts School of Witchcraft and Wizardry...."

– Letter from Professor McGonagall,
Harry Potter and the Philosopher's Stone film

During Harry's years at Hogwarts, Dumbledore watches over and protects him.

Dumbledore gives Harry the Invisibility Cloak, one of the three Deathly Hallows. It had belonged to Harry's father, James.

Dumbledore and Snape protect Harry and other students when Hogwarts is threatened by an escapee from Azkaban, the wizard prison.

Harry and his closest friends, Ron Weasley and Hermione Granger, look up to Dumbledore.

When student Neville Longbottom stands up to Harry, Ron and Hermione, Dumbledore recognizes his bravery before the whole school.

"It takes a great deal of bravery to stand up to your enemies, but a great deal more to stand up to your friends."

– Professor Dumbledore, *Harry Potter and the Philosopher's Stone* film

After Harry witnesses Voldemort's return, Dumbledore is one of the few to believe him. Many wizards, including the Minister for Magic, are too afraid to accept the truth: the Dark Lord is back.

"Dark and difficult times lie ahead. Soon we must all face the choice between what is right and what is easy."

– Professor Dumbledore, *Harry Potter and the Goblet of Fire* film

Harry and his friends form a student group dedicated to learning defensive spells to protect themselves from Dark magic. They name themselves Dumbledore's Army in honour of Professor Dumbledore.

Harry and fellow D.A. member Neville Longbottom practise in the Room of Requirement.

Fighting Dark Forces

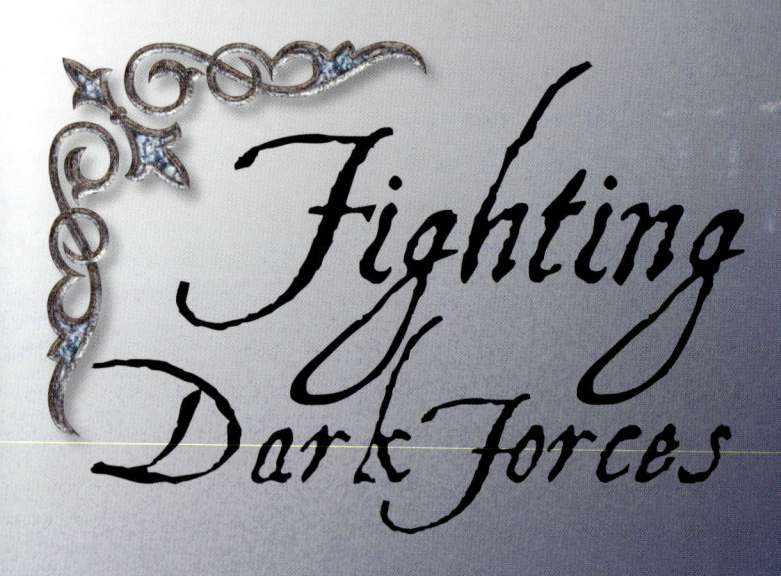

Professor Dumbledore has dedicated his life to protecting witches, wizards and Muggles from the power of Dark magic.

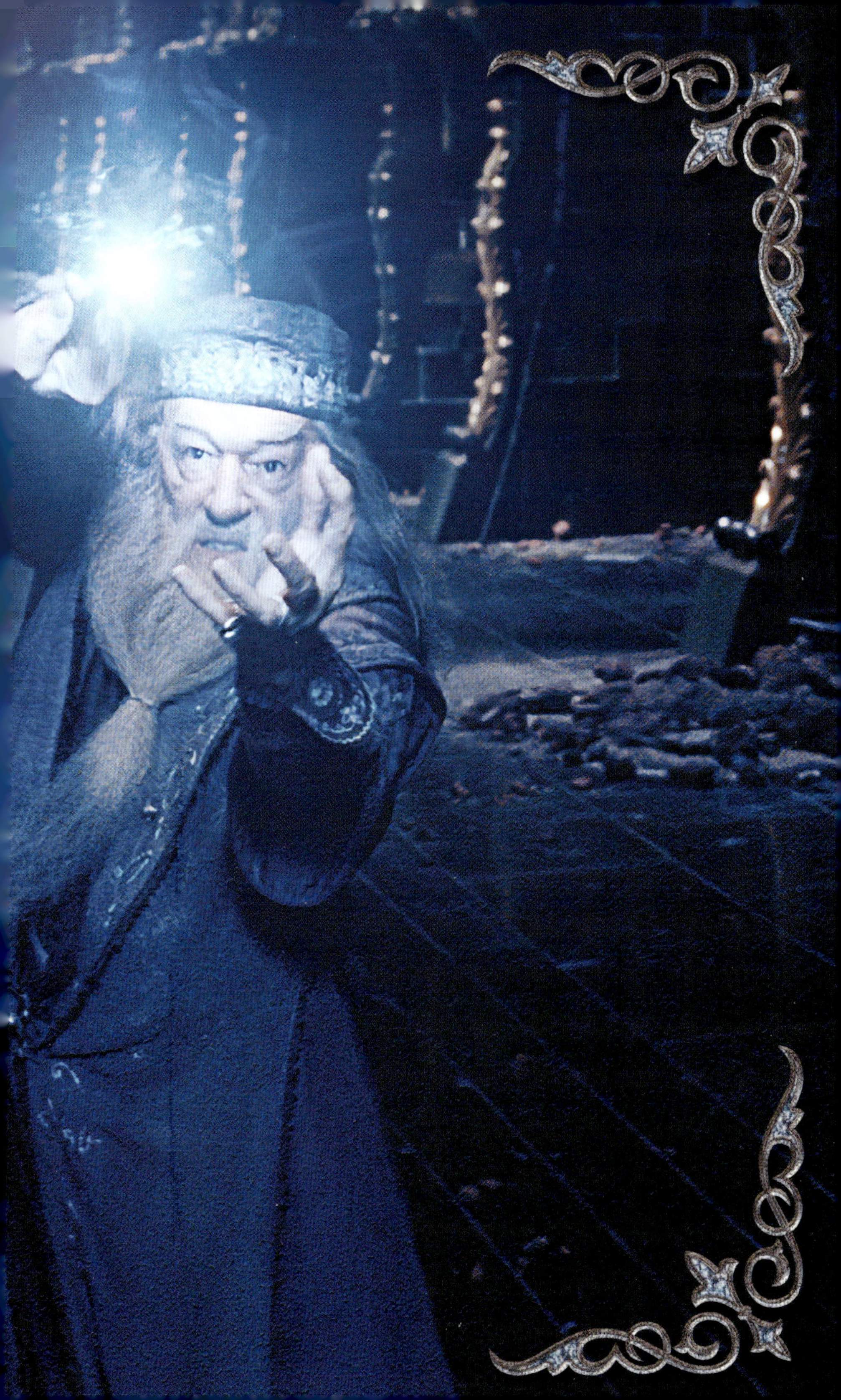

As Voldemort grows stronger, he uses his connection with Harry to lure the boy to the Ministry of Magic. Dumbledore comes to Harry's rescue and duels the Dark Lord.

"It was foolish of you to come here tonight, Tom."

– Professor Dumbledore, *Harry Potter and the Order of the Phoenix* film

Dumbledore is determined to protect Harry from Voldemort.

Dumbledore and Harry discover the secret behind Voldemort's return – in order to become immortal, Voldemort has split his soul and concealed parts of it in objects called Horcruxes. Together, Dumbledore and Harry set out to find and destroy the Horcruxes.

Harry: "If you could find them all… if you did destroy each Horcrux…"

Dumbledore: "One destroys Voldemort."

– Harry Potter and the Half-Blood Prince film

The first Horcrux Dumbledore discovers is a ring that holds a powerful curse.

The Horcrux gravely injures Dumbledore. Professor Snape confines the curse to Dumbledore's hand, but they both know that eventually the curse will spread.

Dumbledore brings Harry to find the next Horcrux, which Voldemort has hidden in a cave.

The Horcrux is protected by Dark magic. Dumbledore must drink a poisonous potion to retrieve it.

The potion weakens Dumbledore, but he still finds the strength to protect Harry from Inferi – corpses that have been reanimated through Dark magic.

When Professor Dumbledore and Harry return to Hogwarts, they find out that Death Eaters have broken into the school. After years of being seemingly loyal to Dumbledore, Snape must now prove himself to be an ally to the Dark forces.

Bellatrix Lestrange leads the Death Eaters into Hogwarts.

"Severus... please..."

– Professor Dumbledore, *Harry Potter and the Half-Blood Prince* film

In order to fulfil a promise to Dumbledore, Professor Snape must cast the Killing Curse and end his old friend's life.

Dumbledore falls from the top of Hogwarts's Astronomy Tower. His sacrifice sets a larger plan in motion.

Harry and his friends mourn the passing of their mentor and friend.

Legacy

After Dumbledore's death, Harry remains determined to complete the task Dumbledore left for him: find and destroy the remaining Horcruxes so that Voldemort will become mortal once more.

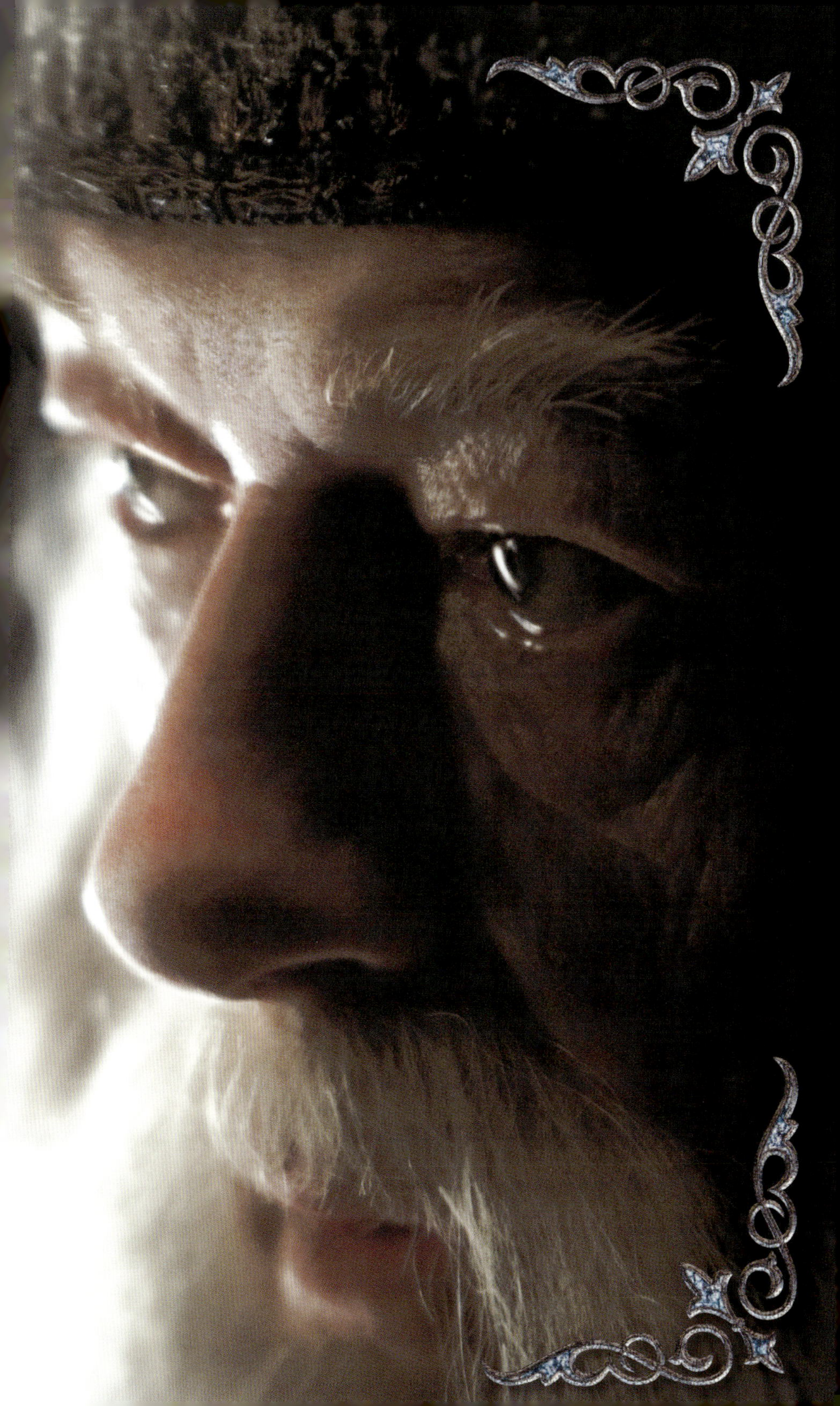

Minister for Magic Rufus Scrimgeour reads Dumbledore's last will and testament to Harry, Ron and Hermione. Dumbledore leaves each of the trio a gift that will serve to help in the hunt for Horcruxes.

Dumbledore leaves Harry the Sword of Gryffindor.

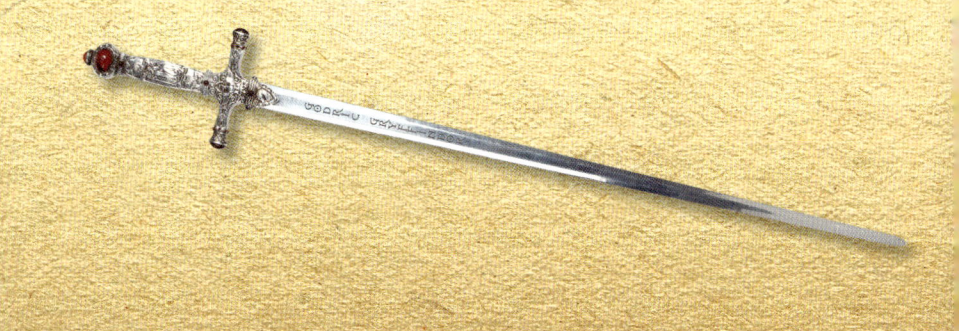

Dumbledore leaves Ron his Deluminator.

Dumbledore leaves Hermione a book that offers information for the quest to defeat the Dark Lord: *The Tales of Beedle the Bard*.

Voldemort becomes convinced he needs a more powerful wand to defeat Harry. He removes the legendary Elder Wand from Dumbledore's tomb.

Voldemort uses the Elder Wand for the first time.

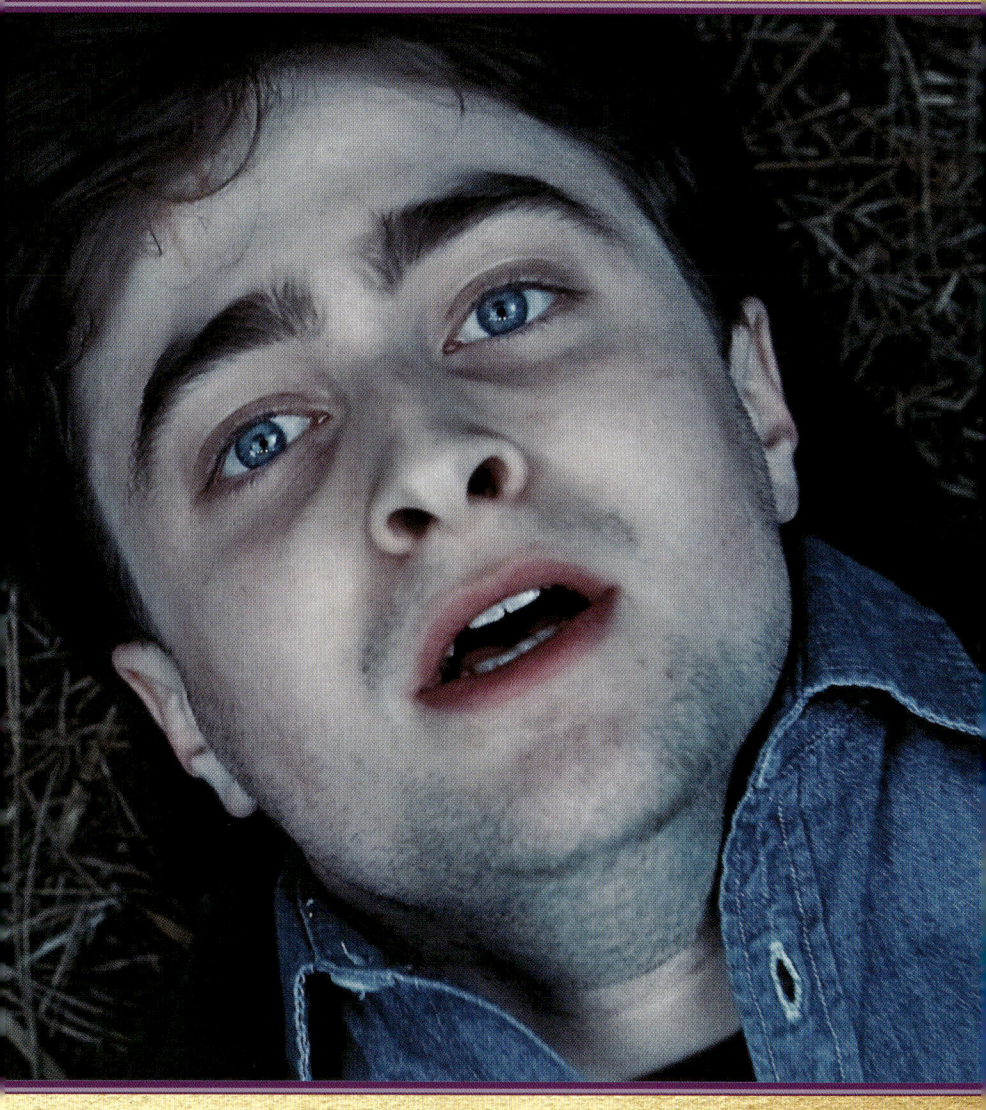

Because of his connection with Voldemort, Harry can sense that the Dark Lord now has the powerful Elder Wand.

Harry, Ron and Hermione discover there are more Horcruxes at Hogwarts.

Dumbledore's younger brother Aberforth and Neville help Harry, Ron and Hermione slip past Death Eaters and back into the castle to find the Horcrux.

There is a secret entrance to the school behind Aberforth's painting of Ariana.

Harry, Ron and Hermione destroy a Horcrux hidden in the Room of Requirement.

Ron and Hermione use a Basilisk fang to destroy another Horcrux in the Chamber of Secrets.

Determined to destroy Harry, Voldemort attacks Hogwarts. During the battle, Voldemort mortally wounds Snape. Just before Snape dies, he tells Harry to take one of his tears to Dumbledore's Pensieve.

When Harry sees Snape's memories, he finally discovers the truth about his connection with Voldemort. Harry himself is a Horcrux. To defeat the Dark Lord, Harry must allow Voldemort to kill him.

Dumbledore: "There's a reason Harry can speak with snakes. There's a reason he can look into Lord Voldemort's mind. A part of Voldemort lives inside him."

Snape: "So when the time comes, the boy must die?"

Dumbledore: "Yes. And Voldemort himself must do it."

– HARRY POTTER AND THE DEATHLY HALLOWS – PART 2 FILM

Harry surrenders himself to Voldemort in the Forbidden Forest. He allows Voldemort to kill him so the Horcrux inside him can be destroyed.

"Harry Potter. The Boy Who Lived. Come to die."

– Voldemort, *Harry Potter and the Deathly Hallows – Part 2* film

Voldemort believes he has killed Harry, but he succeeds only in destroying the Horcrux. As Harry lies unconscious, he has a vision of Dumbledore.

Harry: "So, it's true, then, sir? A part of him lives within me, doesn't it?"

Dumbledore: "Did. It was just destroyed many moments ago by none other than Voldemort himself. . . . You were the Horcrux he never meant to make, Harry."

– HARRY POTTER AND THE DEATHLY HALLOWS – PART 2 FILM

Neville uses the Sword of Gryffindor to destroy the last Horcrux, Voldemort's snake, Nagini.

Thanks to Harry and his friends, Dumbledore's plan has been fulfilled: Voldemort is finally mortal once more. He and Harry can face each other on equal footing.

Harry and Voldemort's final duel at the Battle of Hogwarts.

"Do not pity the dead, Harry. Pity the living and above all, all those who live without love."

– Professor Dumbledore, *Harry Potter and the Deathly Hallows – Part 2* film

Harry Potter

RON WEASLEY

Cinematic Guide

SCHOLASTIC LTD.

Copyright © 2016 Warner Bros. Entertainment Inc.
HARRY POTTER characters, names and related
indicia are © & ™ Warner Bros. Entertainment Inc.
WB SHIELD: ™ & © WBEI.
J.K. ROWLING'S WIZARDING WORLD ™
J.K. Rowling and Warner Bros. Entertainment Inc.
Publishing Rights © JKR. (s16)
SCUS37666

www.harrypotter.com

Scholastic Children's Books
Euston House, 24 Eversholt Street,
London NW1 1DB, UK

A division of Scholastic Ltd
London ~ New York ~ Toronto ~ Sydney ~ Auckland
Mexico City ~ New Delhi ~ Hong Kong

First published in the US by Scholastic Inc, 2016
Published in the UK by Scholastic Ltd, 2016

By Felicity Baker
Art Direction: Rick DeMonico
Page Design: Two Red Shoes Design

ISBN 978 1407 17317 7

Printed and bound by Bell & Bain Ltd, Glasgow

2 4 6 8 10 9 7 5 3 1

All rights reserved

This book is sold subject to the condition that it shall not,
by way of trade or otherwise be lent, resold, hired out, or
otherwise circulated without the publisher's prior consent in
any form or binding other than that in which it is published
and without a similar condition, including this condition,
being imposed upon the subsequent purchaser.

Papers used by Scholastic Children's Books are made from
wood grown in sustainable forests.

www.scholastic.co.uk

Contents

Film Beginnings 4
Life at Hogwarts 10
Family, Friends and Foes 22
Magical Mishaps 36
Quidditch 44
Fighting Dark Forces 50

Film Beginnings

Upon their first meeting, Ron Weasley quickly becomes best friends with Harry Potter. For Ron, attendance at Hogwarts is expected: the Weasleys are a large wizarding family, with Ron the sixth of seven children. Ron's biggest challenge is discovering his own path at school when his many siblings have been there before him.

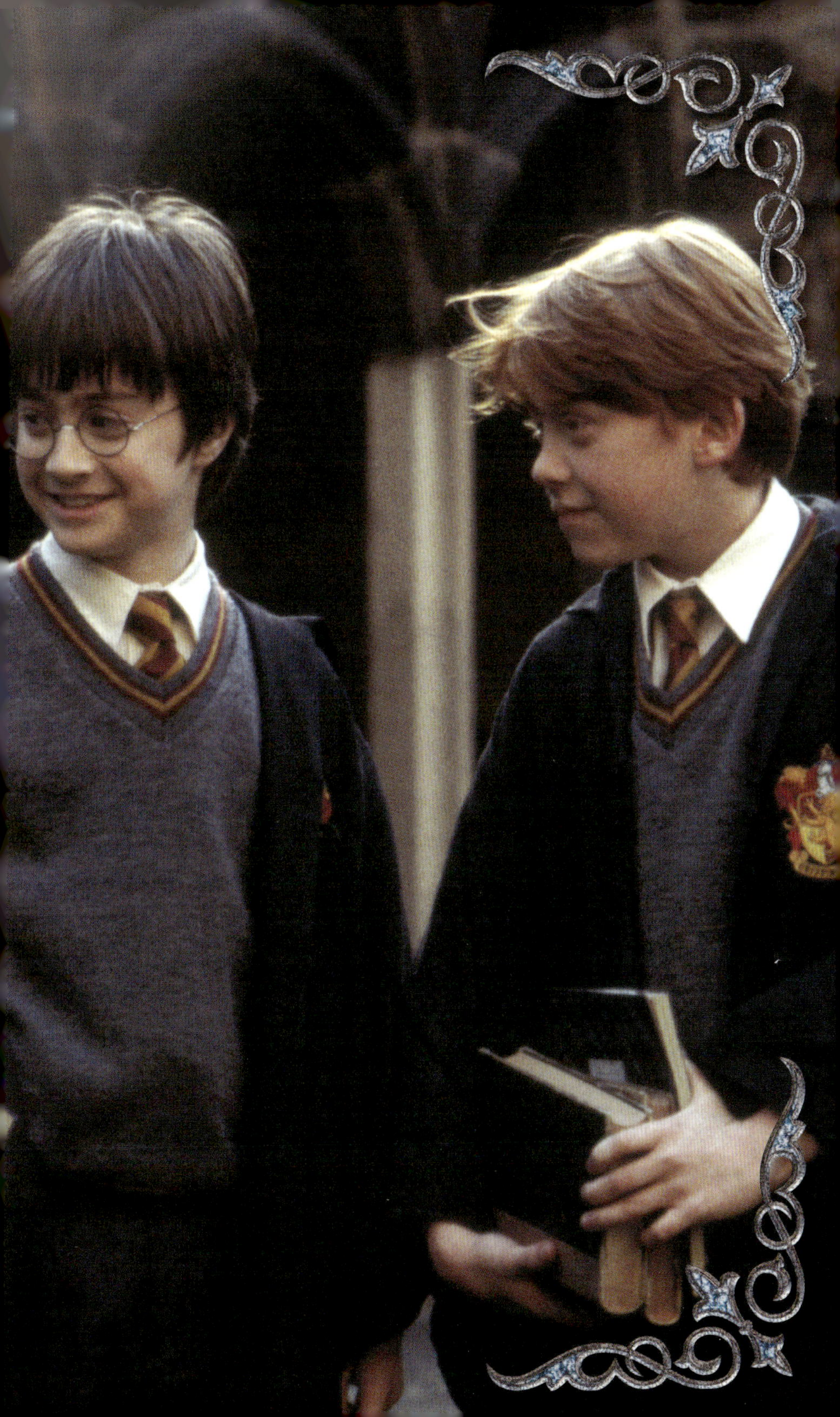

Ron's adventure begins when he arrives at Platform Nine and Three-Quarters in King's Cross station to board the Hogwarts Express for the first time.

> "Now all you've got to do is walk straight at the wall between platforms nine and ten."
>
> – Molly Weasley, *Harry Potter and the Philosopher's Stone* film

Ron's mother and younger sister Ginny come to the train station to see Ron off to Hogwarts.

7

On-board, Ron discovers he's in the same compartment as the famous Harry Potter!

The boys get along right away – and Harry seals the friendship with sweets he buys from the food trolley.

"There's chocolate and peppermint. And there's also spinach, liver and tripe."

– Ron Weasley, on Bertie Bott's Every Flavour Beans, *Harry Potter and the Philosopher's Stone* film

Ron also meets Hermione Granger, another first year, and initially thinks that she's a know-it-all. It's hard to imagine from this first moment that these three young wizards would become best friends!

Life at Hogwarts

Ron fits right in at Hogwarts. Not only does he become close with Harry and Hermione and other Gryffindor students, but he becomes an important part of Harry's adventures.

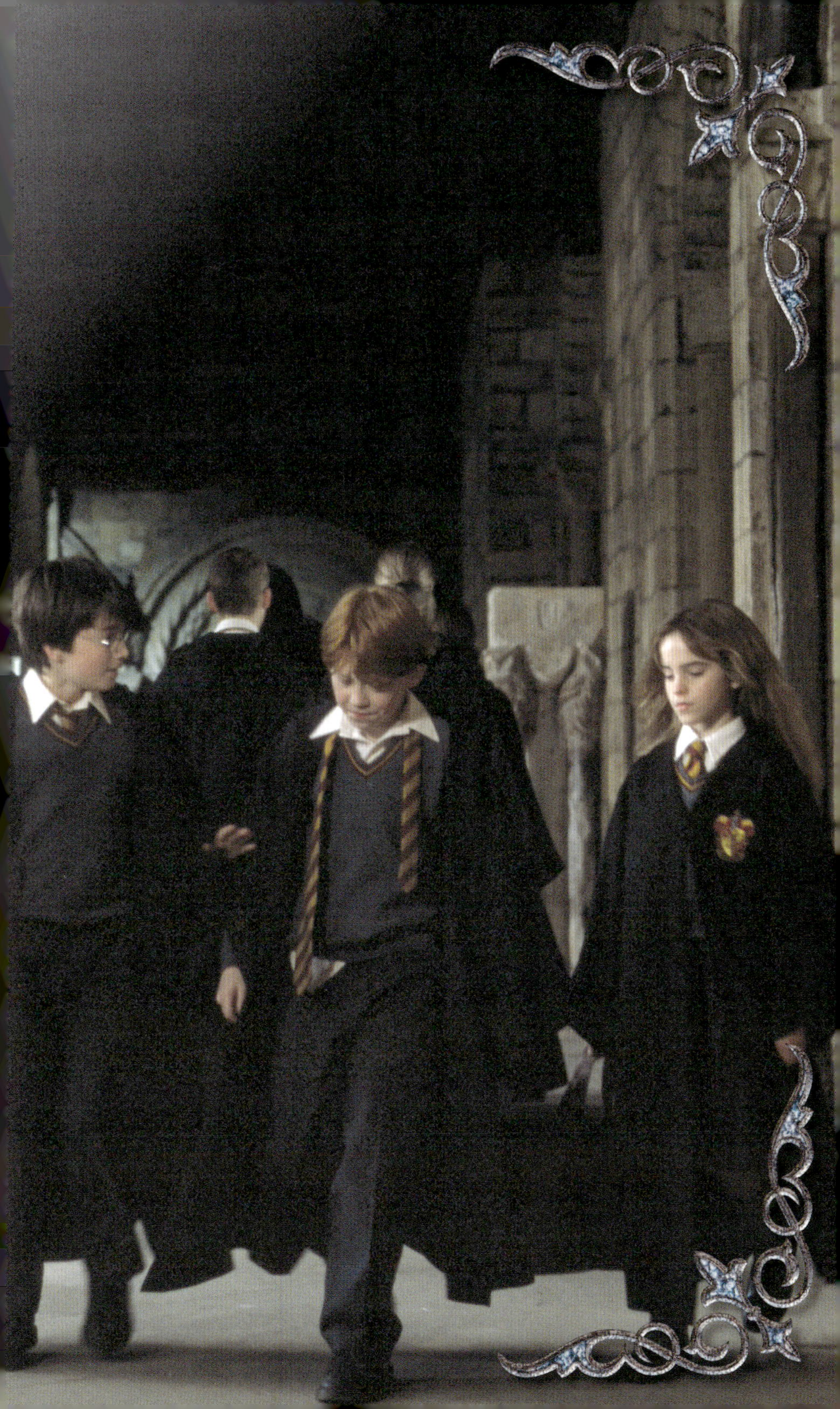

After arriving at Hogwarts, Ron is sorted into Gryffindor house – just like his older brothers.

"Ha! Another Weasley. I know just what to do with you – Gryffindor!"

– The Sorting Hat, Harry Potter and the Philosopher's Stone film

Ron's new friends, Harry and Hermione, are sorted into Gryffindor, too.

Ron and Harry have all their classes together.

Ron and Harry arrive late to their first Transfiguration class with Professor McGonagall.

Ron also has classes with Hermione – much to his dismay, Hermione often tells him what to do.

Ron and his classmates have their first flying lesson with Madam Hooch.

Not all classes are as thrilling as learning to fly. Ron and Harry struggle to pay attention in Professor Trelawney's Divination class.

Earmuffs are needed in Herbology class! Ron unearths a young screaming Mandrake whose cries are damaging, if not quite fatal.

Ron faces his greatest fear during Defence Against the Dark Arts class – a giant spider.

Ron and Hermione encourage Harry to teach their fellow students how to defend themselves against the Dark Arts and start Dumbledore's Army.

The trio creates the secret group to teach defensive magical skills to protect them from Lord Voldemort and other Dark forces.

Life at Hogwarts is not just about classes – there's time for some fun, too.

A trip to Hogsmeade.

Playing wizard chess with Harry.

The Yule Ball, a dance held during the Triwizard Tournament, brings exciting new challenges to Ron and Harry.

Ron and Harry try to work up the courage to ask the beautiful Beauxbatons students to the Yule Ball.

"Mum's sent me a dress."
– Ron Weasley, *Harry Potter and the Goblet of Fire* film

Ron and Harry attend the Yule Ball with the Patil sisters, Padma and Parvati.

Surprising many, including Ron and Harry, Hermione attends with Viktor Krum, a famous Quidditch player from Durmstrang.

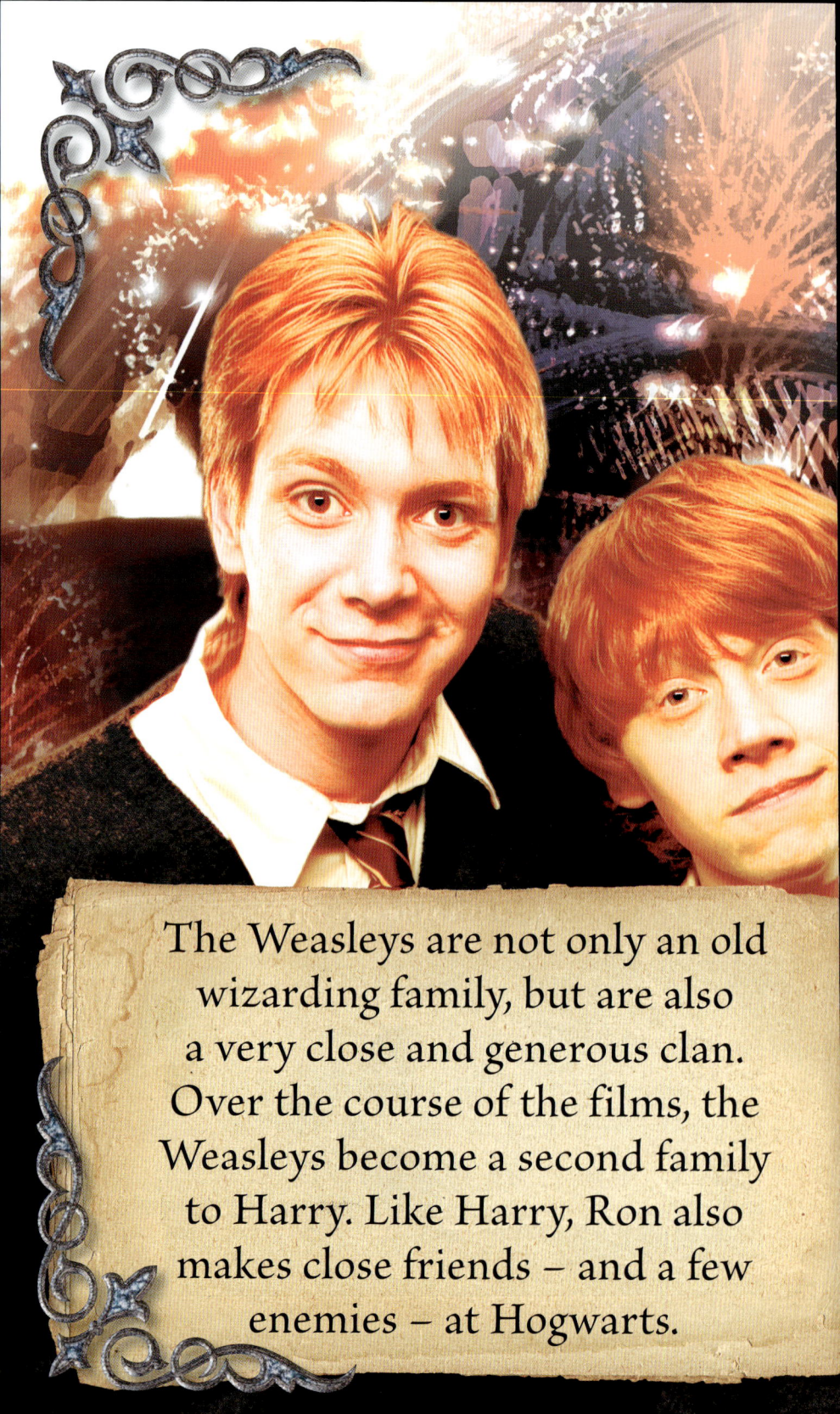

The Weasleys are not only an old wizarding family, but are also a very close and generous clan. Over the course of the films, the Weasleys become a second family to Harry. Like Harry, Ron also makes close friends – and a few enemies – at Hogwarts.

Family, Friends and Foes

The Weasleys live in a magical home called The Burrow.

"It's not much, but it's home."
– Ron Weasley, Harry Potter and the Chamber of Secrets film

Ron's mum and dad, Arthur and Molly Weasley.

There are many Weasleys, and the family has a special clock to keep track of everyone's whereabouts.

Two of Ron's older brothers, Fred and George, are twins. They are notorious at Hogwarts for making mischief.

Fred and George Weasley take an Ageing Potion to make themselves old enough to enter the Triwizard Tournament. This time, their wizardry backfires!

The Weasley twins' fireworks dragon chases Professor Umbridge, one of their least favourite teachers, right out of the Great Hall!

Ron's younger sister, Ginny, is a powerful witch.

Ginny proves to be a helpful ally in the fight against Lord Voldemort.

Ginny takes a special interest in Harry, much to Ron's disapproval.

In addition to the twins, Ron has three more older brothers: Bill, Charlie and Percy.

Bill graduated from Hogwarts before Ron arrived.

Percy, Ron's third-oldest brother, is a prefect at Hogwarts. Unlike Ron, Percy loves having authority and enforcing the rules.

Ron invites his closest friends, Harry and Hermione, to go to the Quidditch World Cup with his family. Their fun is interrupted by Death Eaters.

> "As Minister for Magic, it gives me great pleasure to welcome each and every one of you to the final of the four hundred and twenty-second Quidditch World Cup. Let the match begin!"
>
> – Cornelius Fudge, *Harry Potter and the Goblet of Fire* film

In his sixth year, Ron begins dating fellow Gryffindor Lavender Brown.

Hermione has feelings for Ron and is devastated about Ron's relationship with Lavender.

After Ron drinks poison meant for Professor Dumbledore, Hermione is the first to be by Ron's side – much to Lavender's dismay. Ron calls out for Hermione in his sleep, revealing that he may have strong feelings for her.

Even though Ron is a loyal friend and fun to be around, he does have foes.

The most notorious of them are Draco Malfoy and his cohorts, Crabbe and Goyle.

> *"Red hair and a hand-me-down robe? You must be a Weasley."*
>
> – Draco Malfoy, *Harry Potter and the Philosopher's Stone* film

"Were you in Slytherin and your fate rested with me, the both of you would be on the train home tonight."

– Professor Snape, *Harry Potter and the Chamber of Secrets* film

Professor Snape appears to dislike Ron almost as much as he dislikes Harry, and he threatens to expel them both from Hogwarts more than once.

Magical Mishaps

From the very beginning, Ron has his ups and downs learning to perform magic. His adventures in the wizarding world often turn quickly into *mis*adventures.

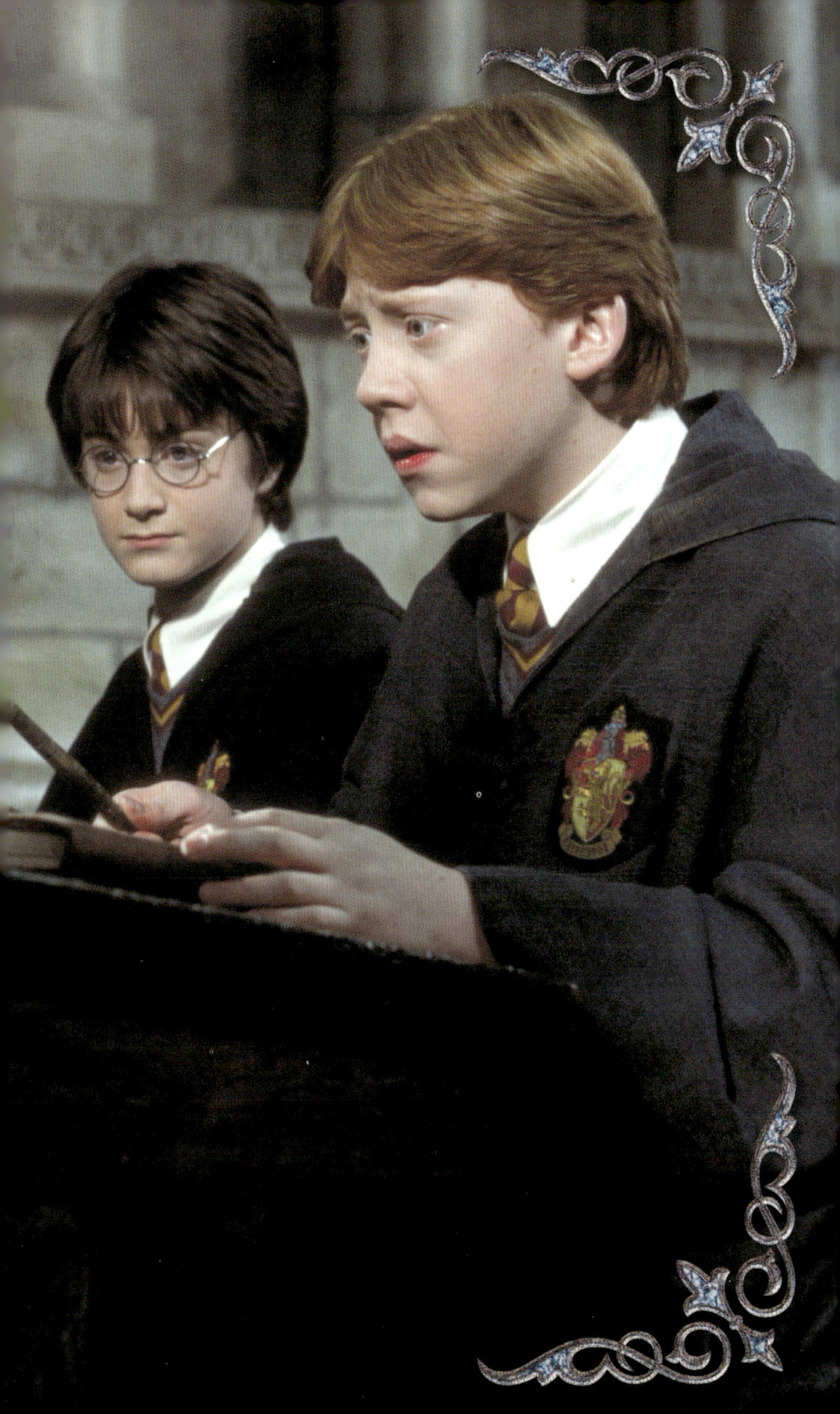

After Harry and Ron miss the train to Hogwarts at the start of their second year, the boys find a way to get to school: Mr Weasley's flying car!

"Ron. I should tell you. Most Muggles aren't accustomed to seeing a flying car."

– Harry Potter, *Harry Potter and the Chamber of Secrets* film

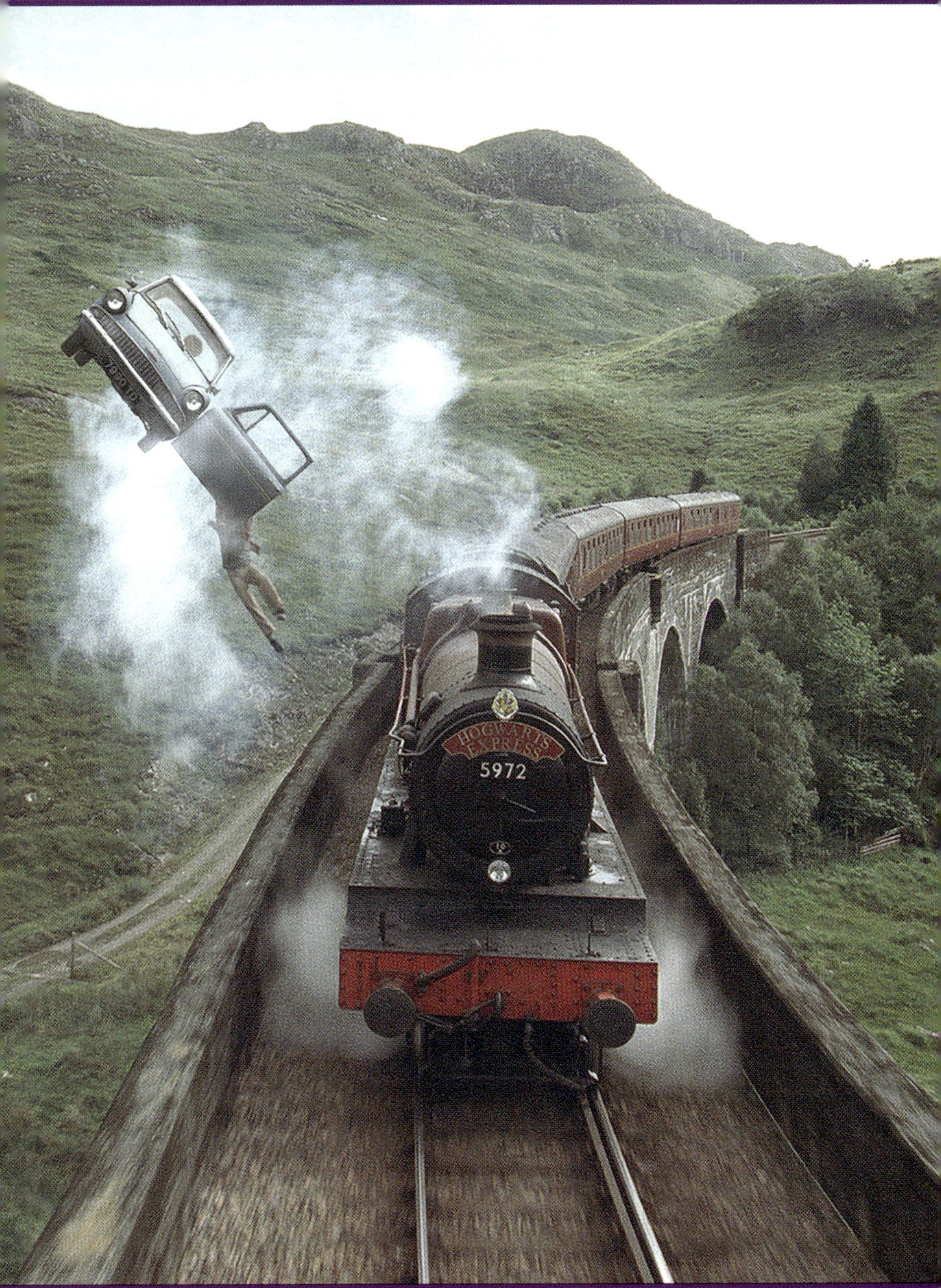
HOGWARTS EXPRESS
5972

The flying car, with Ron and Harry inside, crash-lands into the Whomping Willow on the grounds at Hogwarts.

Mrs Weasley sends Ron a Howler – an angry letter that scolds him in front of the whole school.

"RONALD WEASLEY! How dare you steal that car? I am absolutely disgusted!"

– Mrs Weasley's Howler, *Harry Potter and the Chamber of Secrets* film

Sometimes Ron's magical mishaps range from the disgusting to the ridiculous.

Ron's wand breaks after the car crashes. He tries to fix it, but it never quite works the same way.

After Draco insults Hermione, Ron tries to curse him. But the spell goes wrong, and Ron ends up vomiting slugs.

Ron accidentally eats chocolates laced with a love potion that was meant for Harry. As a result, Ron becomes hopelessly lovesick for Romilda Vane.

Ron: "It's no joke! I'm in love with her!"

Harry: "Alright, fine, you're in love with her! Have you ever actually met her?"

– HARRY POTTER AND THE HALF-BLOOD PRINCE FILM

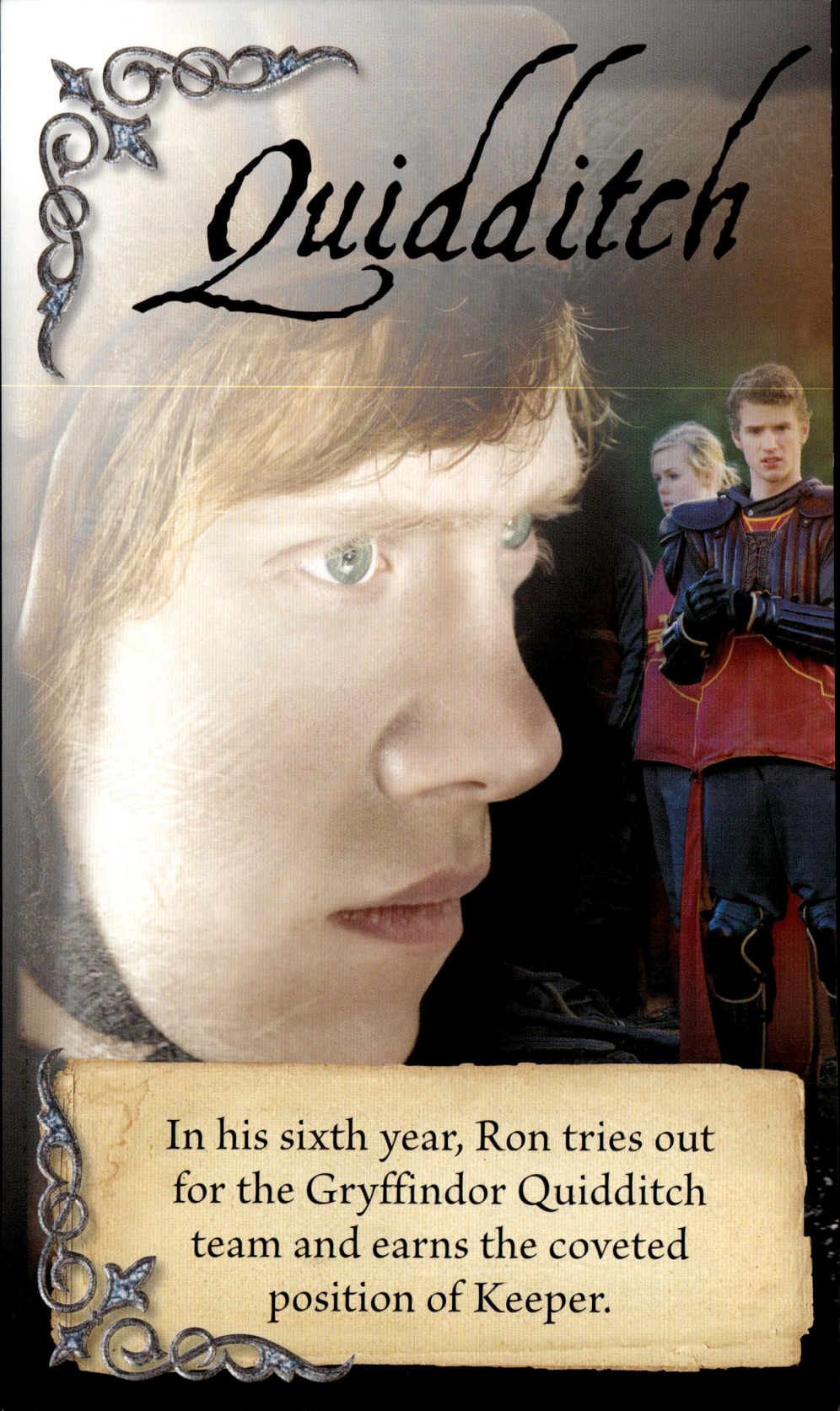

Quidditch

In his sixth year, Ron tries out for the Gryffindor Quidditch team and earns the coveted position of Keeper.

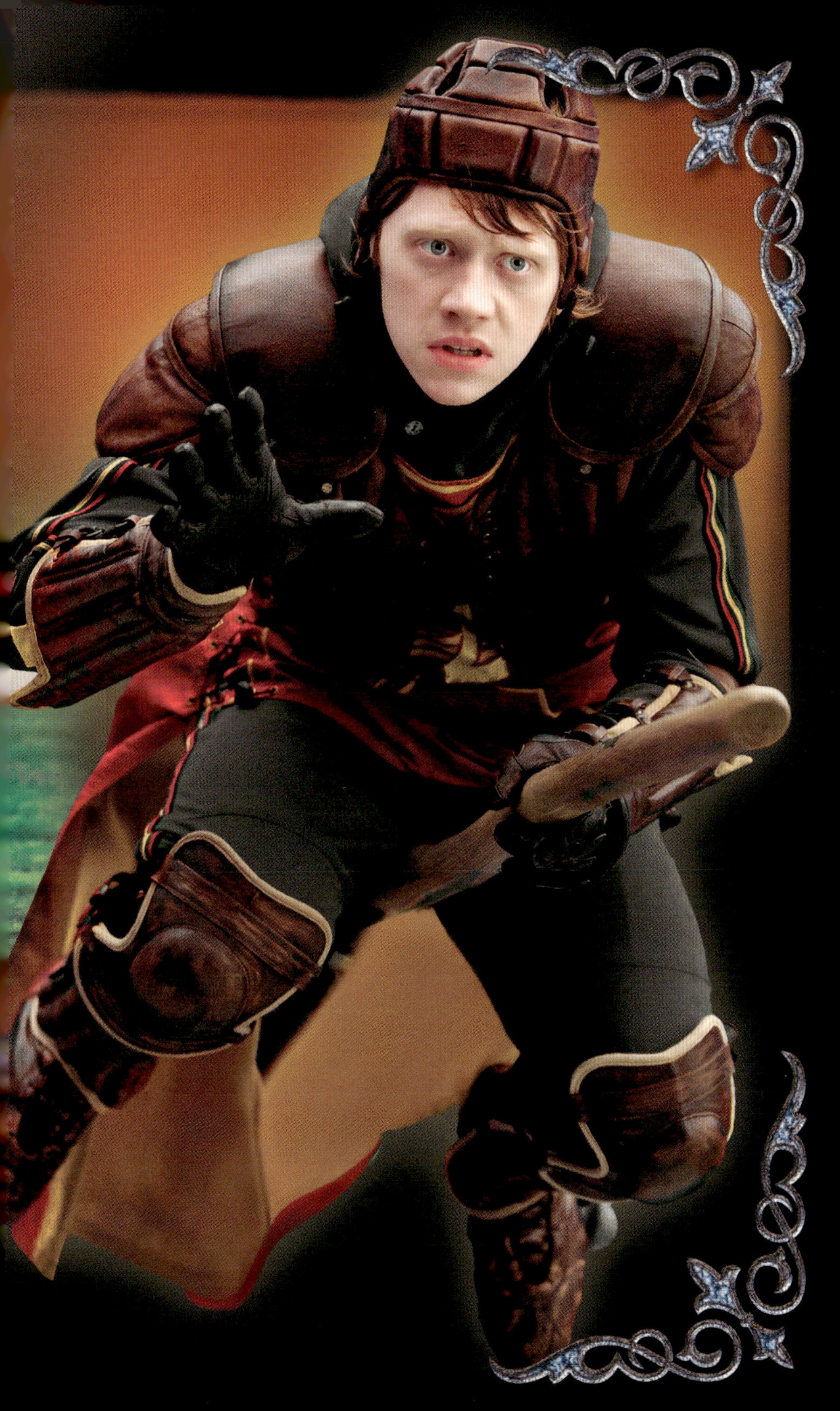

Ron in his Keeper's uniform and gear.

During Quidditch tryouts, Ron makes some daring saves at the goalpost.

In his first Quidditch game, Ron makes a great save! Gryffindor wins!

The Quidditch crowd goes wild for Ron!

Post-game celebration for Ron in the Gryffindor common room.

Fighting Dark Forces

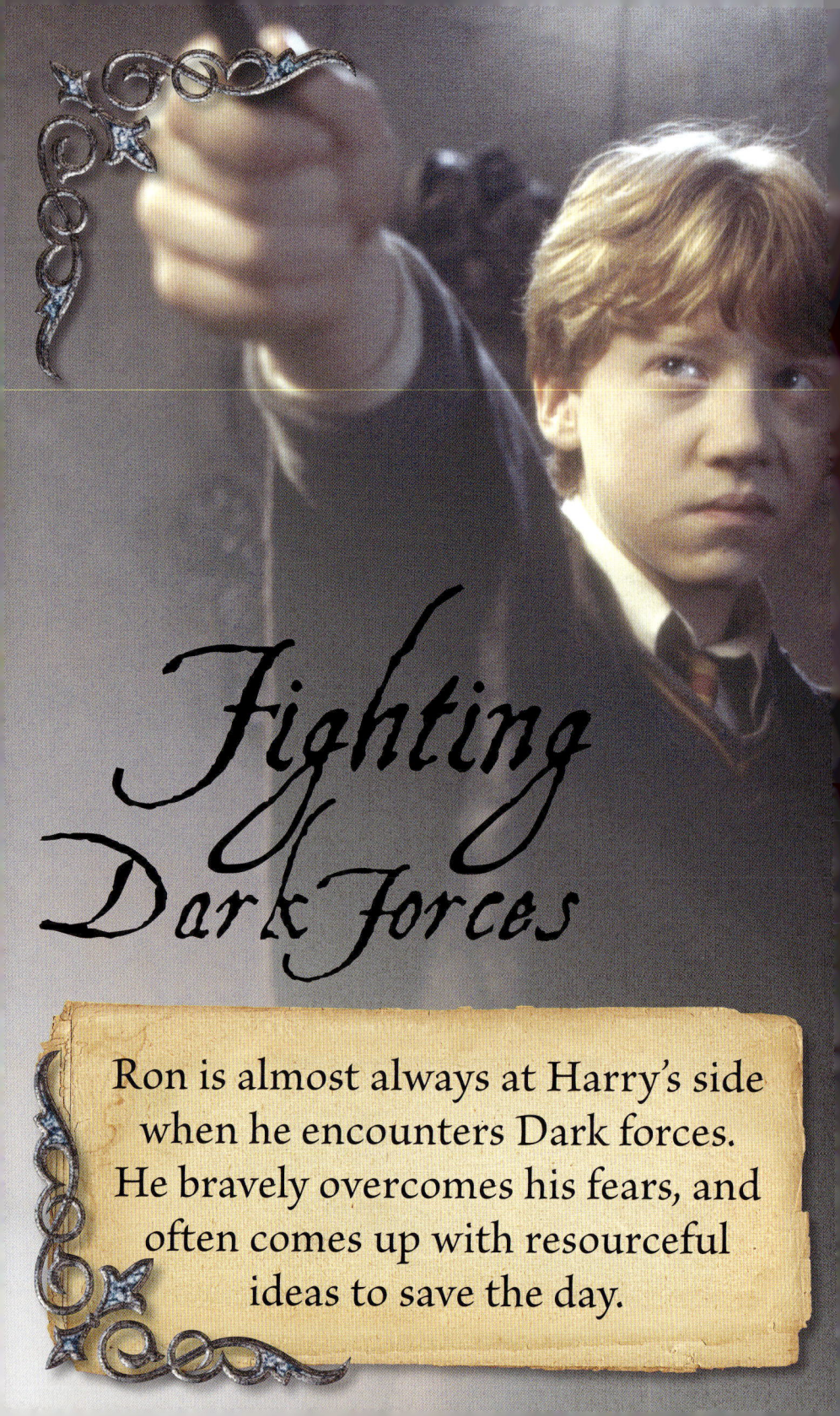

Ron is almost always at Harry's side when he encounters Dark forces. He bravely overcomes his fears, and often comes up with resourceful ideas to save the day.

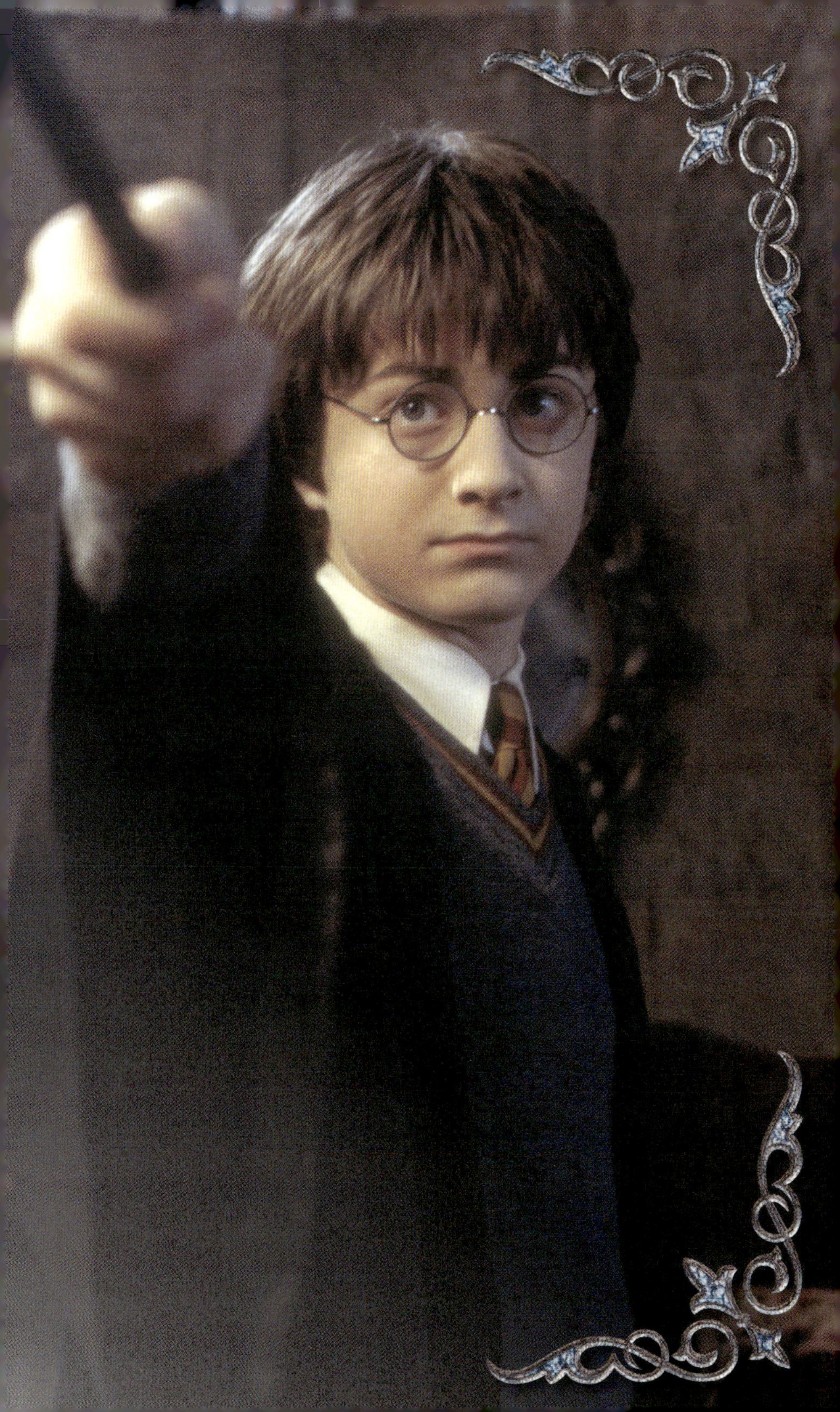

In the first film, Ron, Harry and Hermione search Hogwarts for the Philosopher's Stone. Ron plays a dangerous game of wizard chess in order to help Harry reach the legendary stone.

"You understand, right, Harry? Once I make my move, the queen will take me. Then you're free to check the king."

– Ron Weasley, *Harry Potter and the Philosopher's Stone* film

In his third year, Ron learns the scary truth about Scabbers, his pet rat – he's not really a rat at all!

Scabbers turns out to be Peter Pettigrew, one of Lord Voldemort's Death Eaters, in disguise!

Since Ron's parents are in the Order of the Phoenix, a group dedicated to stopping Voldemort, the whole Weasley family – and those associated with them – are in constant danger.

Nagini, Voldemort's snake, attacks Arthur Weasley.

Death Eaters attack The Burrow.

Harry, Ron and Hermione go on their most dangerous mission yet – the hunt for Horcruxes.

Voldemort has concealed parts of his soul in these bewitched objects and creatures. If the trio destroys the Horcruxes, they can then destroy Voldemort. Ron, Harry and Hermione plan to steal a Horcrux during a raid on the Ministry of Magic.

At the Ministry, Dolores Umbridge has a locket that is one of Voldemort's Horcruxes.

Ron, Harry and Hermione steal the locket, but its evil is so powerful that it drives Ron mad enough to abandon his friends.

Ron gets out from under the influence of the Horcrux locket and returns to help his friends.

He saves Harry from drowning in a lake and then uses the Sword of Gryffindor to destroy the locket.

Hermione is furious at Ron for leaving her and Harry at a desperate time.

Ron: "How long do you reckon she'll stay mad at me?"

Harry: "Just keep talking 'bout that little ball of light touching your heart – she'll come 'round."

– Harry Potter and the Deathly Hallows – Part 1 film

On their hunt for Horcruxes, Snatchers kidnap Ron, Harry and Hermione and bring them to Malfoy Manor, Draco's family home.

Ron uses his Deluminator, a gift from Dumbledore, to turn off the lights so he and Harry can ambush the Death Eaters.

Ron and Harry rescue Hermione from being tortured by Bellatrix Lestrange and escape with Luna Lovegood, Ollivander the wandmaker and the Goblin Griphook.

During the final battle against Voldemort at Hogwarts, Ron and Hermione become closer than ever.

After Ron and Hermione destroy another Horcrux, they embrace, admitting their feelings for each other at last.

Ron: "Do you think we'll ever have a quiet year at Hogwarts?"

Harry & Hermione: "No."

Ron: "Yeah, didn't think so. Oh well, what's life without a few dragons?"

– HARRY POTTER AND THE GOBLET OF FIRE FILM

Harry Potter

HARRY POTTER

Cinematic Guide

SCHOLASTIC LTD.

Copyright © 2016 Warner Bros. Entertainment Inc.
HARRY POTTER characters, names and related
indicia are © & ™ Warner Bros. Entertainment Inc.
WB SHIELD: ™ & © WBEI.
J.K. ROWLING'S WIZARDING WORLD ™
J.K. Rowling and Warner Bros. Entertainment Inc.
Publishing Rights © JKR. (s16)
SCUS37664

www.harrypotter.com

Scholastic Children's Books
Euston House, 24 Eversholt Street,
London NW1 1DB, UK

A division of Scholastic Ltd
London ~ New York ~ Toronto ~ Sydney ~ Auckland
Mexico City ~ New Delhi ~ Hong Kong

First published in the US by Scholastic Inc, 2016
Published in the UK by Scholastic Ltd, 2016

By Felicity Baker
Art Direction: Rick DeMonico
Page Design: Two Red Shoes Design

ISBN 978 1407 17315 3

Printed and bound by Bell & Bain Ltd, Glasgow

2 4 6 8 10 9 7 5 3 1

All rights reserved

This book is sold subject to the condition that it shall not,
by way of trade or otherwise be lent, resold, hired out, or
otherwise circulated without the publisher's prior consent in
any form or binding other than that in which it is published
and without a similar condition, including this condition,
being imposed upon the subsequent purchaser.

Papers used by Scholastic Children's Books are made from
wood grown in sustainable forests.

www.scholastic.co.uk

Contents

Film Beginnings 4
Life at Hogwarts 20
Family, Friends and Foes 36
Beasts and Creatures 50
Battling Voldemort 58

Film Beginnings

Harry Potter always thought he was an ordinary boy. But on his eleventh birthday, Harry finds out a wonderful secret – he's a wizard!

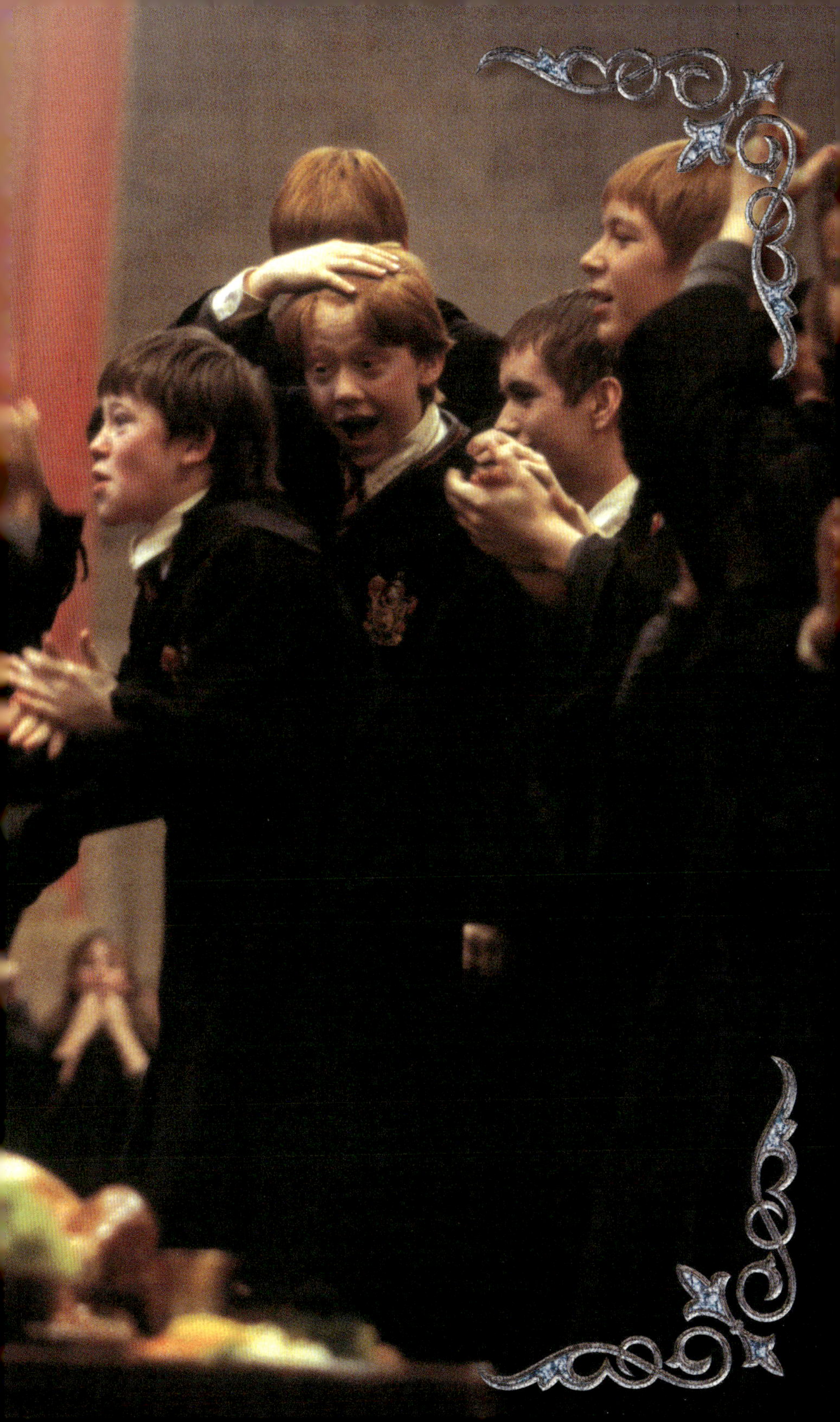

Harry Potter's parents, Lily and James, meet at Hogwarts School of Witchcraft and Wizardry when they are students. They fall in love and eventually get married.

Lily before she starts school at Hogwarts.

James as a Hogwarts student.

When Harry is just a baby, his parents are killed by the evil Lord Voldemort. He tries to kill Harry, too. Harry survives with a lightning bolt scar on his forehead as a terrible reminder.

Professors Dumbledore and McGonagall, wizard friends of Harry's parents, bring baby Harry to live with his Muggle relatives, the Dursleys.

Rubeus Hagrid, a wizard and gamekeeper at Hogwarts, brings baby Harry to Privet Drive by flying motorcycle.

Aunt Petunia, Uncle Vernon and Harry's cousin, Dudley, are horribly mean to Harry.

They never tell Harry the truth about his parents' past.

Harry lives in a cupboard under the stairs.

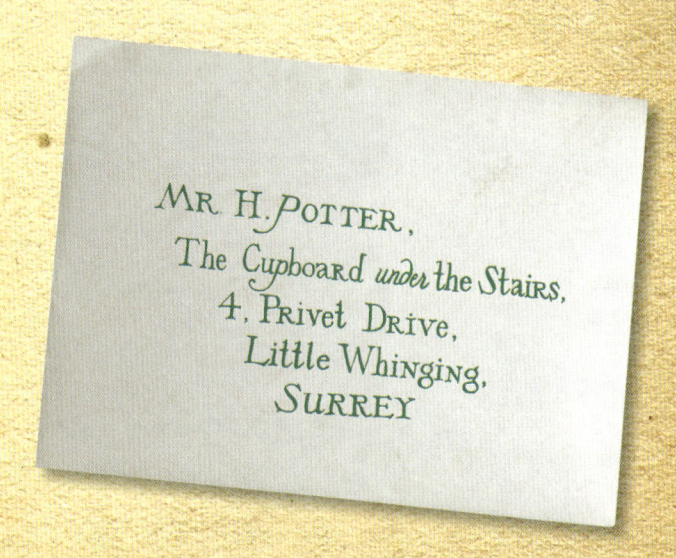

> Mr. H. Potter,
> The Cupboard under the Stairs,
> 4, Privet Drive,
> Little Whinging,
> Surrey

They don't even give Harry a vitally important piece of post – a letter from Hogwarts School of Witchcraft and Wizardry, inviting him to attend the school.

But Harry's destiny cannot be hindered. The Dursleys are unable to hide the letters from Harry forever.

"Dear Mr Potter, we are pleased to inform you that you have been accepted at Hogwarts School of Witchcraft and Wizardry..."

– Letter from Professor McGonagall, *Harry Potter and the Philosopher's Stone* film

Harry meets Hagrid again when he comes to take the boy away to his new life at Hogwarts.

Hagrid tells Harry the truth about his parents.

Hagrid takes Harry to Diagon Alley, a place where witches and wizards shop.

Hagrid and Harry go to Gringotts, a wizards' bank run by goblins, to get the money Harry's parents left him.

Then they go to Ollivanders to buy Harry a wand.

"It is curious that you should be destined for this wand when its brother... gave you that scar."

– Mr Ollivander, *Harry Potter and the Philosopher's Stone* film

To get to Hogwarts, Harry must take the Hogwarts Express from Platform Nine and Three-Quarters at King's Cross station. At the station, Harry meets another boy who is a first year at Hogwarts, Ron Weasley.

"Can you tell me where I might find Platform Nine and Three-Quarters?"

– Harry Potter, *Harry Potter and the Philosopher's Stone* film

9¾ HOGWARTS EXPRESS

Ron's mother tells Harry if he's nervous, he may find it easier to get onto Platform Nine and Three-Quarters if he gets a running start.

Ron and Harry get to know each other on the ride to Hogwarts.

Ron: "So, so, is it true? I mean, do you really have the... the...?"

Harry: "The what?"

Ron: "The scar."

– HARRY POTTER AND THE PHILOSOPHER'S STONE film

Later, they are joined by fellow first year, Hermione Granger.

Hermione casts a spell that fixes Harry's broken glasses.

Life at Hogwarts

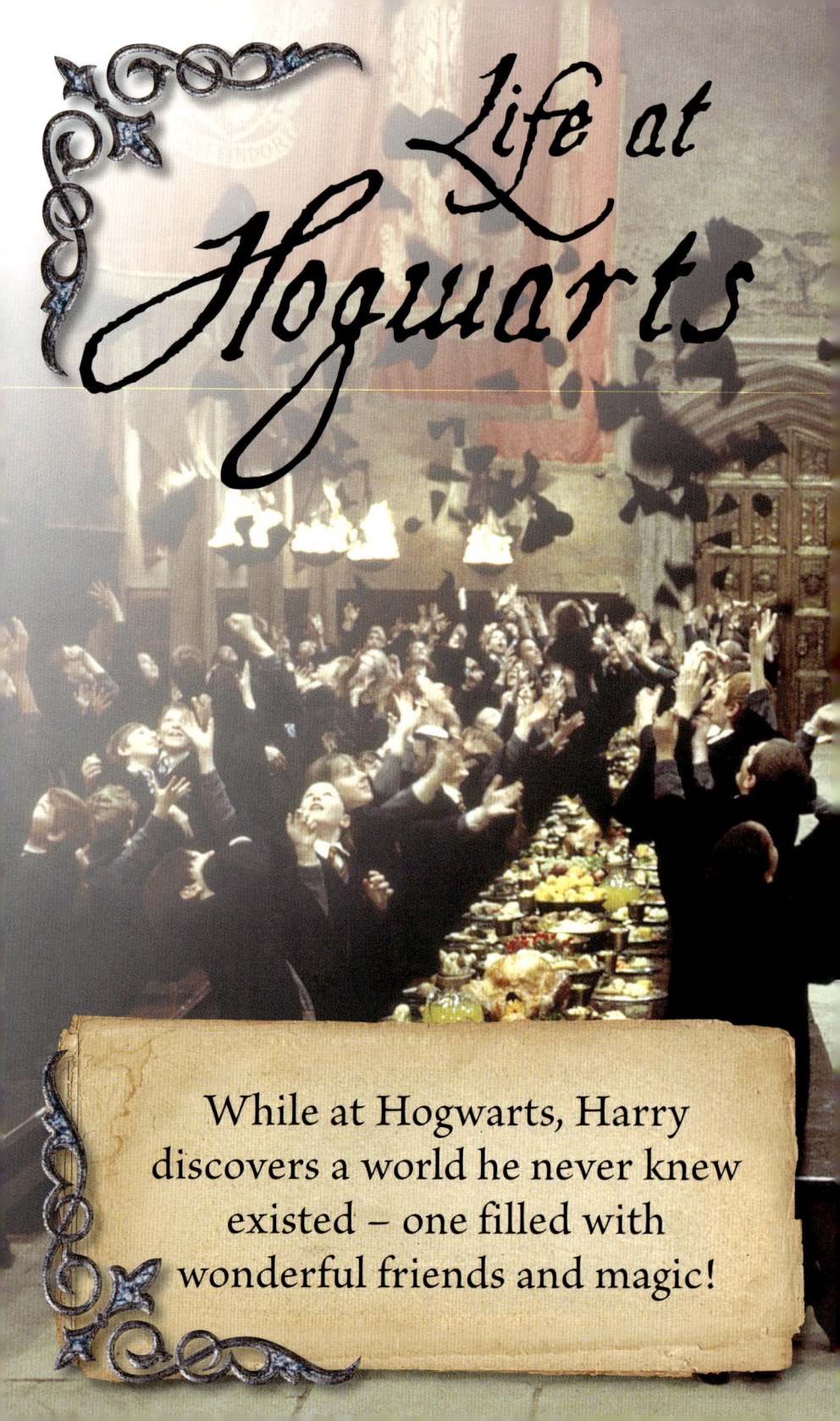

While at Hogwarts, Harry discovers a world he never knew existed – one filled with wonderful friends and magic!

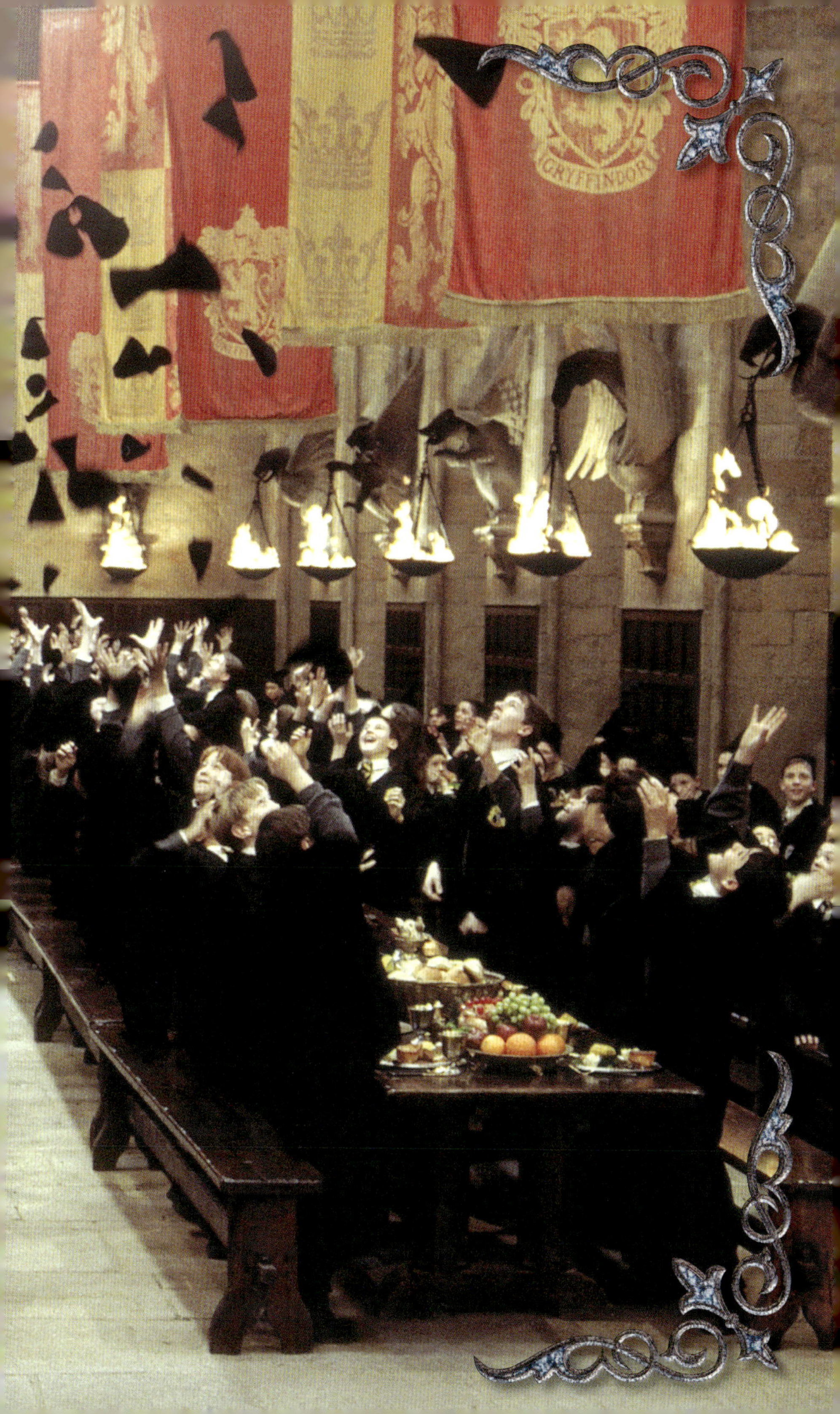
GRYFFINDOR

When students first arrive at Hogwarts, they gather in the Great Hall to be sorted into their houses by the Sorting Hat.

"You must be sorted into your houses. They are Gryffindor, Hufflepuff, Ravenclaw and Slytherin. Now while you are here, your house will be like your family."

– PROFESSOR MCGONAGALL, *HARRY POTTER AND THE PHILOSOPHER'S STONE* FILM

Harry is sorted into Gryffindor, just as both his parents had been.

His new friends are sorted into Gryffindor, too.

Hogwarts is filled with many enchanted and mysterious objects and creatures.

Fred and George Weasley give Harry the Marauder's Map. It shows the location of every person inside Hogwarts.

Professor Dumbledore gives Harry something special that belonged to his father – an Invisibility Cloak.

While exploring an off-limits room at Hogwarts, Harry stumbles upon the Mirror of Erised. In it, he sees the smiling faces of his parents.

> *"It shows us nothing more or less than the deepest and most desperate desires of our hearts."*
>
> – Professor Dumbledore, *Harry Potter and the Philosopher's Stone* film

Classes at Hogwarts are nothing like regular school – they're always exciting, and often challenging.

Harry dreads going to Professor Snape's Potions class. It always seems to Harry as if Snape is out to get him.

Herbology class is taught by Professor Sprout.

Students try to see the future in Professor Trelawney's Divination class.

In flying lessons, Harry discovers his natural talent on a broomstick.

When the students are faced with the threat of Lord Voldemort, Harry secretly teaches his friends how to protect themselves. This group becomes known as Dumbledore's Army.

"Every great wizard in history has started out as nothing more than what we are now – students. If they can do it, why not us?"

– Harry Potter, *Harry Potter and the Order of the Phoenix* film

The Triwizard Tournament is a magical contest that takes place between Hogwarts, the Durmstrang Institute and Beauxbatons Academy of Magic. Harry is selected as a contestant for Hogwarts.

The First Task is to retrieve a golden egg guarded by a dragon.

In the Second Task, Harry has to save Ron from the bottom of a black lake, dodging vicious merpeople along the way.

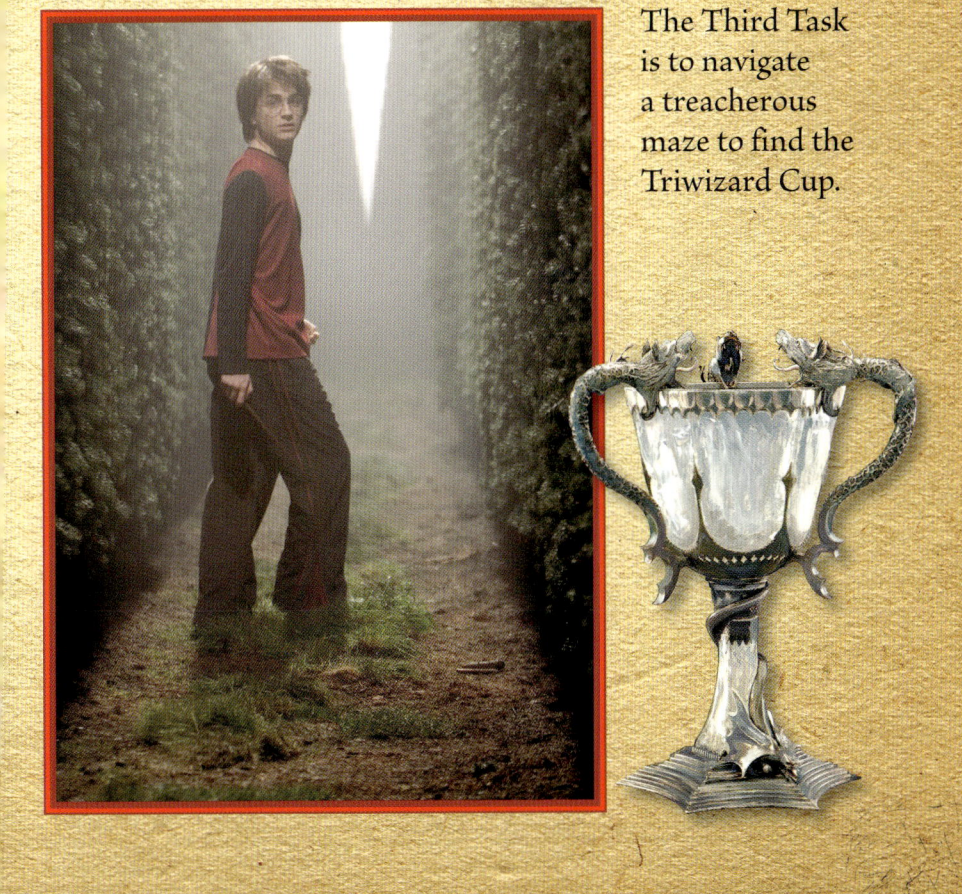

The Third Task is to navigate a treacherous maze to find the Triwizard Cup.

Harry works hard at Hogwarts, but still takes time to have fun and attend special parties.

Harry dances with fellow Gryffindor Parvati Patil at the Yule Ball.

Harry enjoys playing wizard chess with Ron.

Hermione, Harry and Ron visit Hogsmeade on weekends.

There is no pastime Harry enjoys more than Quidditch.

Professor McGonagall recruits Harry to be the Seeker for Gryffindor.

Harry looks up to Gryffindor's Quidditch Captain and Keeper, Oliver Wood.

Harry faces his rival Draco Malfoy on the Quidditch pitch.

Quidditch is a tough sport – even tougher when Dementors attack during a match.

Family, Friends and Foes

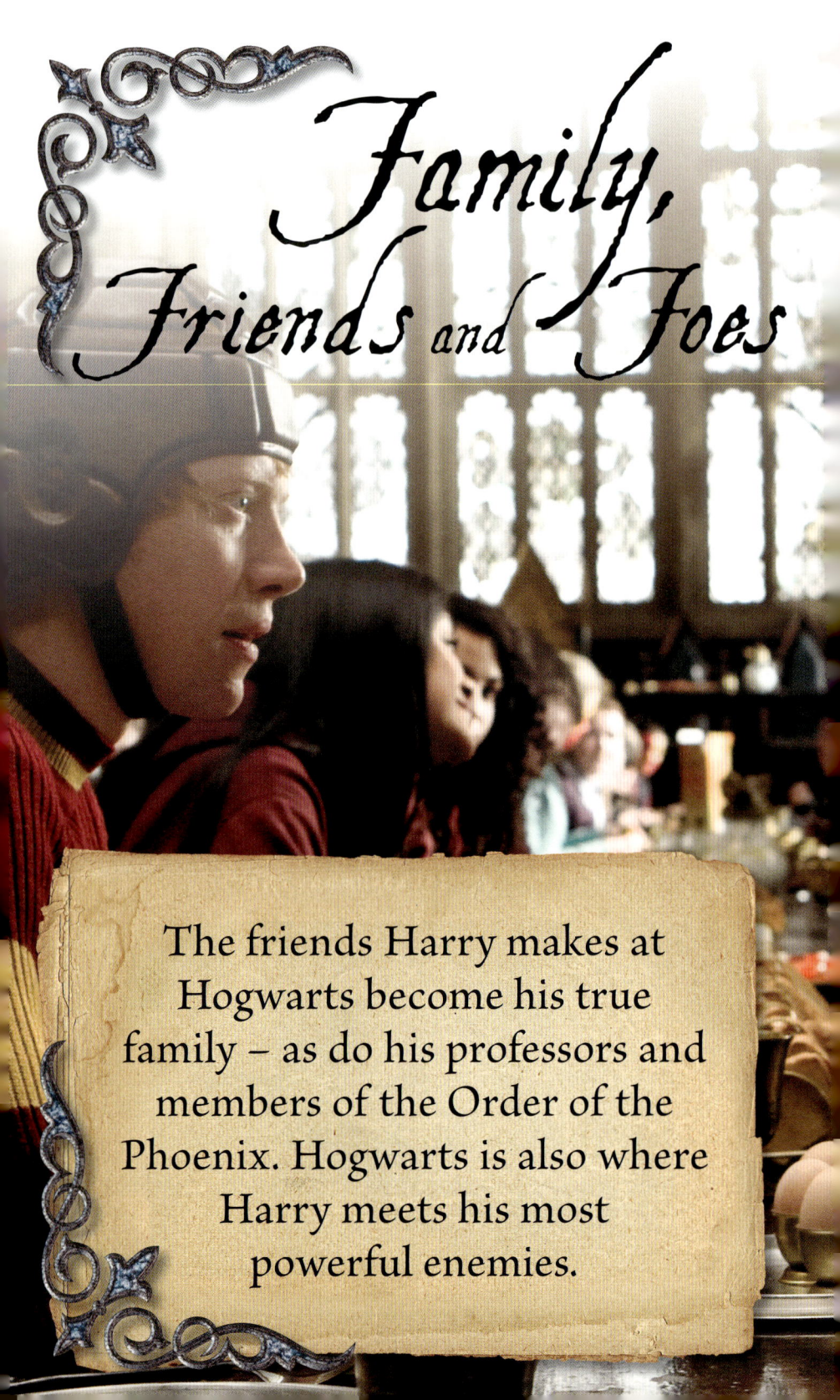

The friends Harry makes at Hogwarts become his true family – as do his professors and members of the Order of the Phoenix. Hogwarts is also where Harry meets his most powerful enemies.

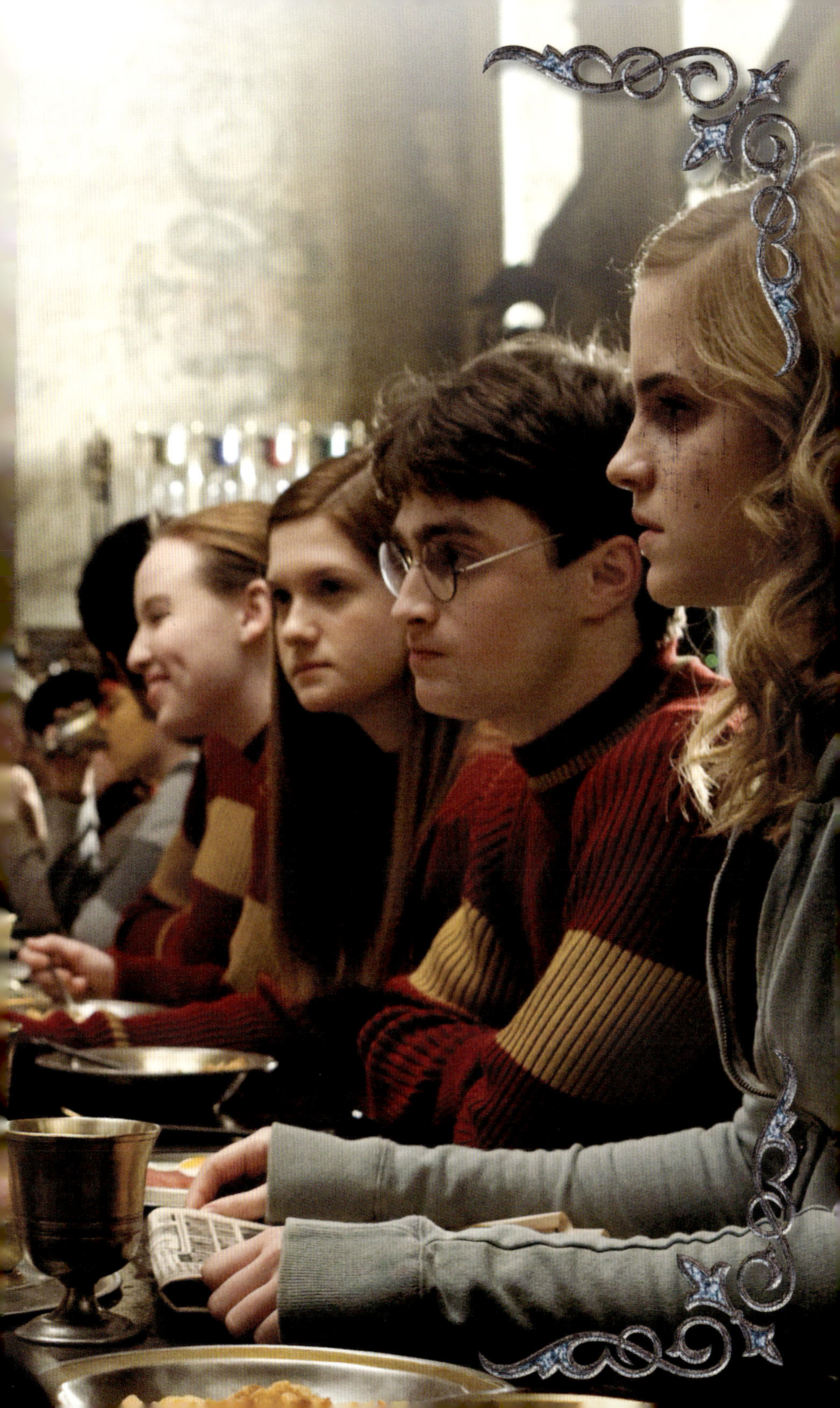

Harry, Ron and Hermione form a bond that is truly unbreakable.

"Maybe you don't have to do this all by yourself, mate."

– Ron Weasley, Harry Potter and the Order of the Phoenix film

"We wouldn't last two days without her... Don't tell her I said that."

– Ron Weasley about Hermione Granger, *Harry Potter and the Deathly Hallows – Part 2* film

"You need us, Harry."

– Hermione Granger, *Harry Potter and the Half-Blood Prince* film

Harry's extended family grows during his time at Hogwarts.

In his third year, Harry discovers he has a godfather, Sirius Black.

The Weasleys treat Harry as if he is family.

Harry accompanies the Weasleys to the Quidditch World Cup.

The Order of the Phoenix, a group of wizards that oppose Lord Voldemort, embraces Harry. Many of the members are Harry's most trusted allies including Professor Dumbledore, Professor McGonagall and Professor Lupin.

Albus Dumbledore

Minerva McGonagall

Kingsley Shacklebolt

Nymphadora Tonks

Remus Lupin

Rubeus Hagrid

Sirius Black

Alastor "Mad-Eye" Moody

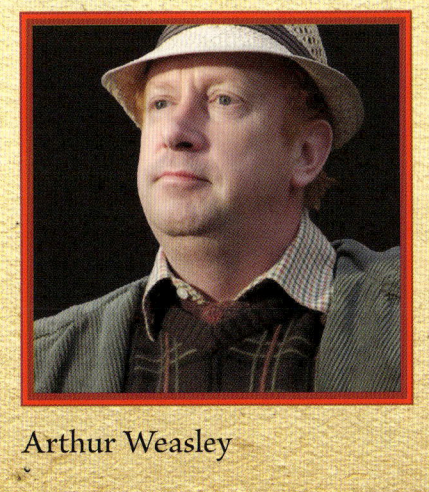

Arthur Weasley

Molly Weasley

Neville Longbottom often plays a part in Harry's adventures.

> "Things we lose have a way of coming back to us in the end. If not always in the way we expect."
>
> – Luna Lovegood, Harry Potter and the Order of the Phoenix film

Harry becomes friends with Ravenclaw student, Luna Lovegood.

Cho Chang, a Ravenclaw, becomes close to Harry when she joins Dumbledore's Army. They even share a kiss in Harry's fifth year.

Harry and Ginny Weasley become more than friends.

Some professors are more interested in being nasty to Harry than teaching him.

Professor Snape appears to loathe Harry.

"Clearly fame isn't everything, is it, Mr Potter?"

– Professor Snape, *Harry Potter and the Philosopher's Stone* film

Professor Dolores Umbridge, a Defence Against the Dark Arts teacher, treats Harry harshly. She punishes Harry by making him use a special quill that scars his hand.

From the moment Harry and Draco Malfoy meet, there is bad blood between them. This hatred extends to Malfoy's parents who are Death Eaters.

"There's not a witch or wizard who went bad who wasn't in Slytherin."

– Ron Weasley, *Harry Potter and the Philosopher's Stone* film

Lord Voldemort was once a student at Hogwarts known as Tom Riddle. Voldemort believes from the Prophecy that Harry is strong enough to defeat him, and therefore wants Harry dead.

"The Prophecy said neither one can live while the other one survives. It means one of us is going to have to kill the other in the end."

– Harry Potter, Harry Potter and the Order of the Phoenix film

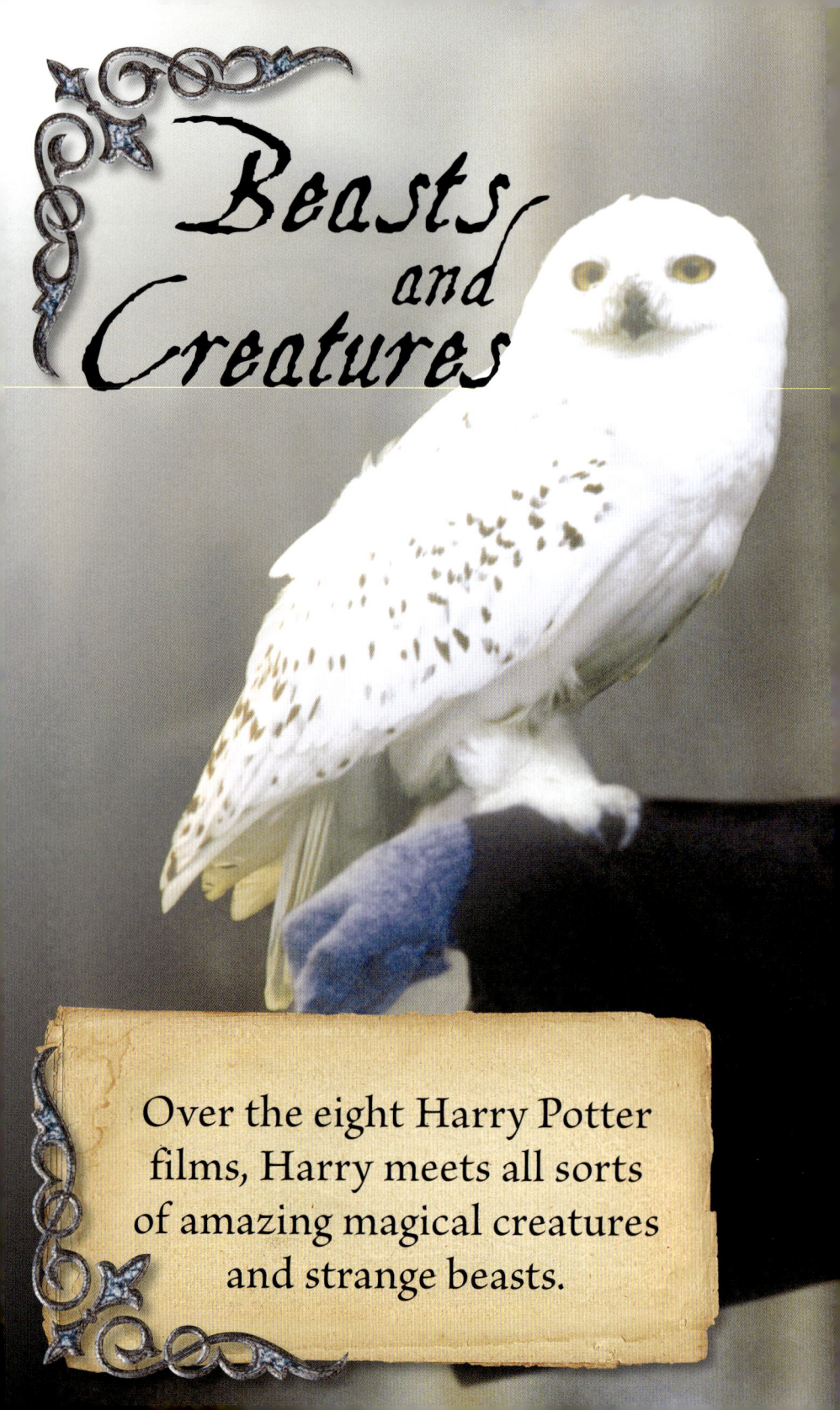

Beasts and Creatures

Over the eight Harry Potter films, Harry meets all sorts of amazing magical creatures and strange beasts.

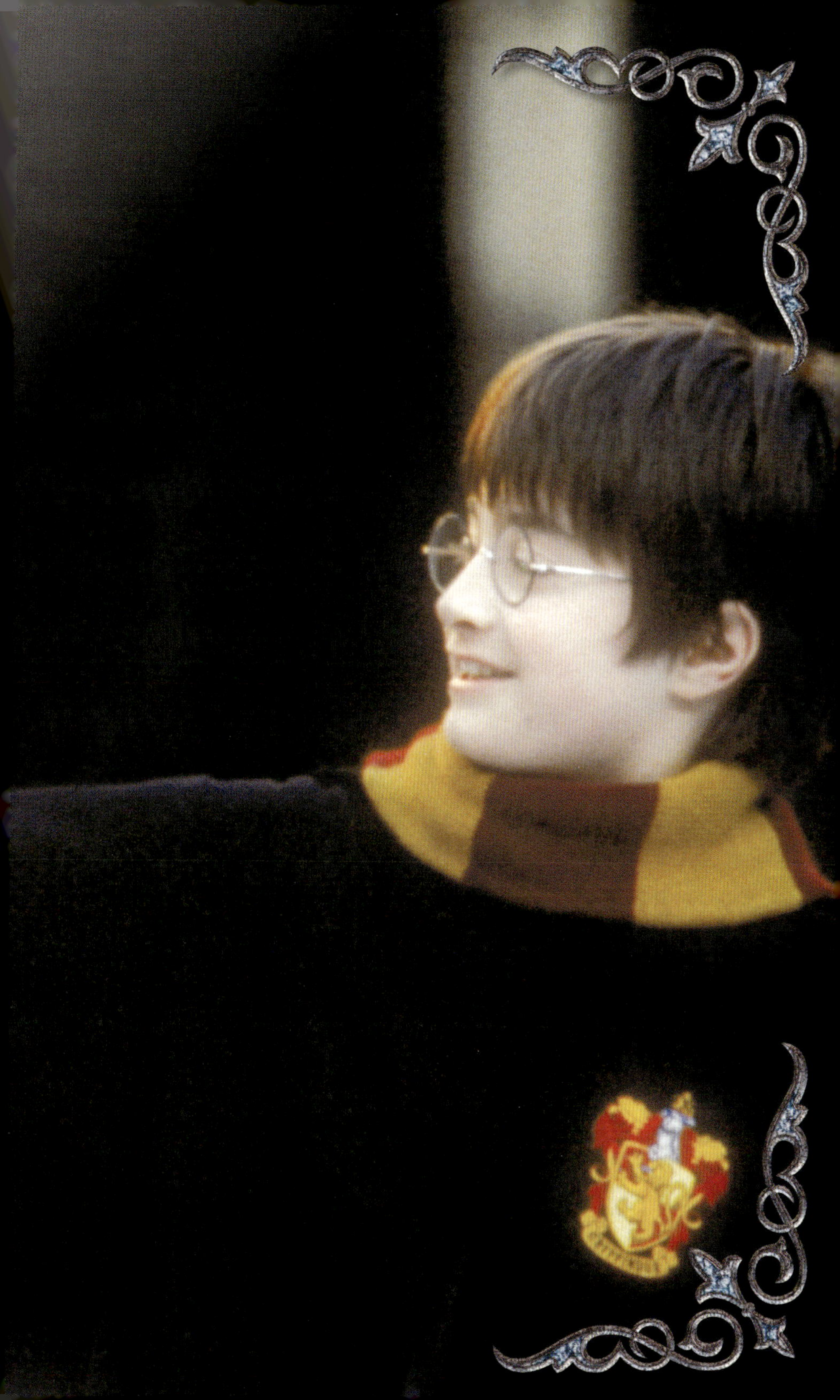

A few magical creatures become Harry's trusted friends and allies.

Harry's snowy owl, Hedwig, is a gift from Hagrid.

Dobby the house-elf befriends Harry and tries his best to help him on a number of occasions.

> "Dobby has come to rescue Harry Potter, of course."
> – Dobby, Harry Potter and the Deathly Hallows – Part 1 film

Harry tricks Lucius Malfoy into releasing Dobby from slavery.

Harry also meets magical creatures that belong to his professors at Hogwarts.

Fawkes, Professor Dumbledore's Phoenix, comes to Harry's aid while he's in the Chamber of Secrets.

"Of course, Phoenix tears have healing powers."

– Harry Potter, *Harry Potter and the Chamber of Secrets* film

Hagrid and Harry with Aragog, Hagrid's beloved pet spider.

Harry with Buckbeak, Hagrid's Hippogriff.

Some creatures that Harry encounters come in handy for making a daring exit. Harry, Ron and Hermione escape Gringotts on the back of a dragon.

> "*Brilliant. Absolutely brilliant.*"
>
> – Ron Weasley, Harry Potter and the Deathly Hallows – Part 2 film

Battling Voldemort

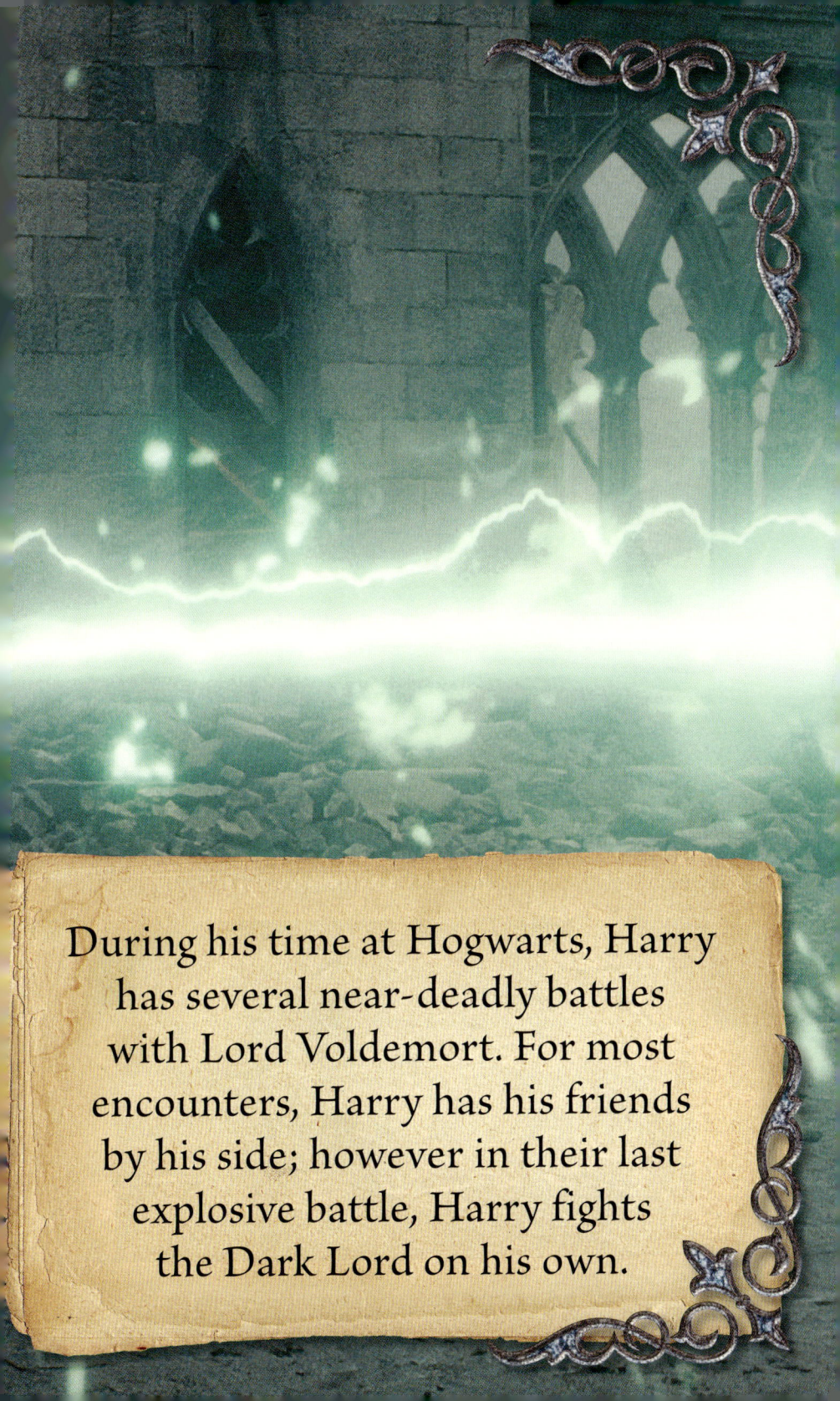

During his time at Hogwarts, Harry has several near-deadly battles with Lord Voldemort. For most encounters, Harry has his friends by his side; however in their last explosive battle, Harry fights the Dark Lord on his own.

During the Third Task of the Triwizard Tournament, Harry and Voldemort come face to face in their first duel. Harry barely escapes with his life.

In Harry's fifth year, Dumbledore intervenes just as Voldemort is about to kill Harry. They have an explosive duel in the Ministry of Magic.

Harry and Voldemort's final battle takes place at Hogwarts.

"Come on, Tom. Let's finish this the way we started it – together."

– Harry Potter to Voldemort, Harry Potter and the Deathly Hallows – Part 2 Film

Once the final Horcrux is destroyed, Voldemort weakens.

Now Harry is finally able to destroy Voldemort once and for all.

"Working hard is important, but there's something that matters even more. Believing in yourself."

— Harry Potter, Harry Potter and the Order of the Phoenix film

Harry Potter

HERMIONE GRANGER

Cinematic Guide

SCHOLASTIC LTD.

Copyright © 2016 Warner Bros. Entertainment Inc.
HARRY POTTER characters, names and related
indicia are © & ™ Warner Bros. Entertainment Inc.
WB SHIELD: ™ & © WBEI.
J.K. ROWLING'S WIZARDING WORLD ™
J.K. Rowling and Warner Bros. Entertainment Inc.
Publishing Rights © JKR. (s16)
SCUS37665

www.harrypotter.com

Scholastic Children's Books
Euston House, 24 Eversholt Street,
London NW1 1DB, UK

A division of Scholastic Ltd
London ~ New York ~ Toronto ~ Sydney ~ Auckland
Mexico City ~ New Delhi ~ Hong Kong

First published in the US by Scholastic Inc, 2016
Published in the UK by Scholastic Ltd, 2016

By Felicity Baker
Art Direction: Rick DeMonico
Page Design: Two Red Shoes Design

ISBN 978 1407 17316 0

Printed and bound by Bell & Bain Ltd, Glasgow

2 4 6 8 10 9 7 5 3 1

All rights reserved

This book is sold subject to the condition that it shall not,
by way of trade or otherwise be lent, resold, hired out, or
otherwise circulated without the publisher's prior consent in
any form or binding other than that in which it is published
and without a similar condition, including this condition,
being imposed upon the subsequent purchaser.

Papers used by Scholastic Children's Books are made from
wood grown in sustainable forests.

www.scholastic.co.uk

Contents

Film Beginnings 4
Life at Hogwarts 10
Family, Friends and Foes 26
Cleverest Moments 40
Fighting Dark Forces 56

Film Beginnings

Hermione Granger grew up in a Muggle family who were proud when she got her letter from Hogwarts. From the moment she boarded the Hogwarts Express as a first year, she showed a talent for magic and spellwork.

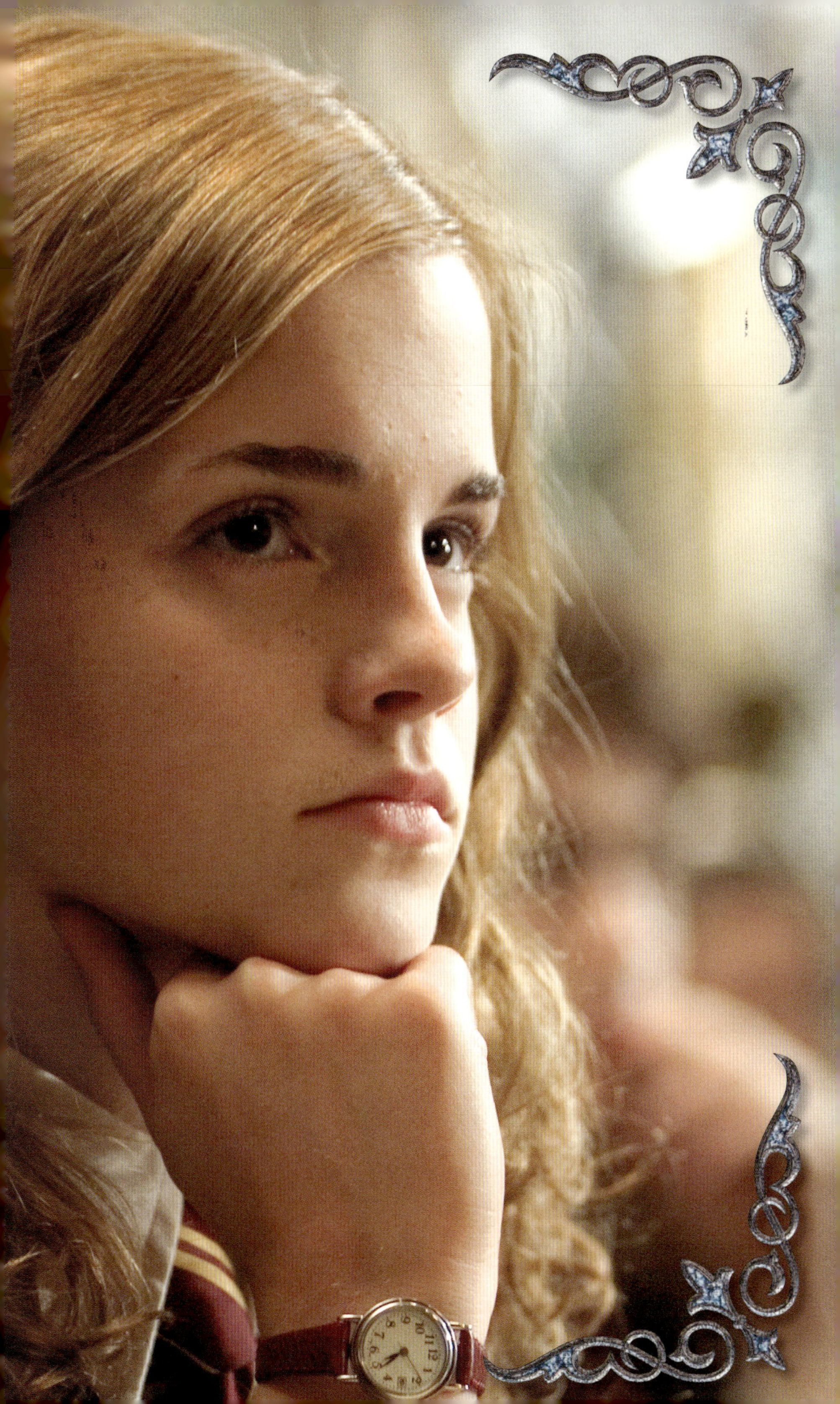

In the first Harry Potter film, Hermione meets Harry and Ron on the Hogwarts Express, a train that brings students from King's Cross station in London to Hogwarts castle at the start of each school year.

HOGWARTS EXPRESS 9¾

"You're Harry Potter, aren't you?
I know all about you, of course."

– Hermione Granger, Harry Potter
and the Philosopher's Stone film

Hermione makes quite an impression when she enters Ron and Harry's train compartment.

Hermione casts a spell to fix Harry's broken glasses with the words "Oculus Reparo."

Hermione and all the other first-year students disembark from the train and take boats across the lake to get to Hogwarts castle.

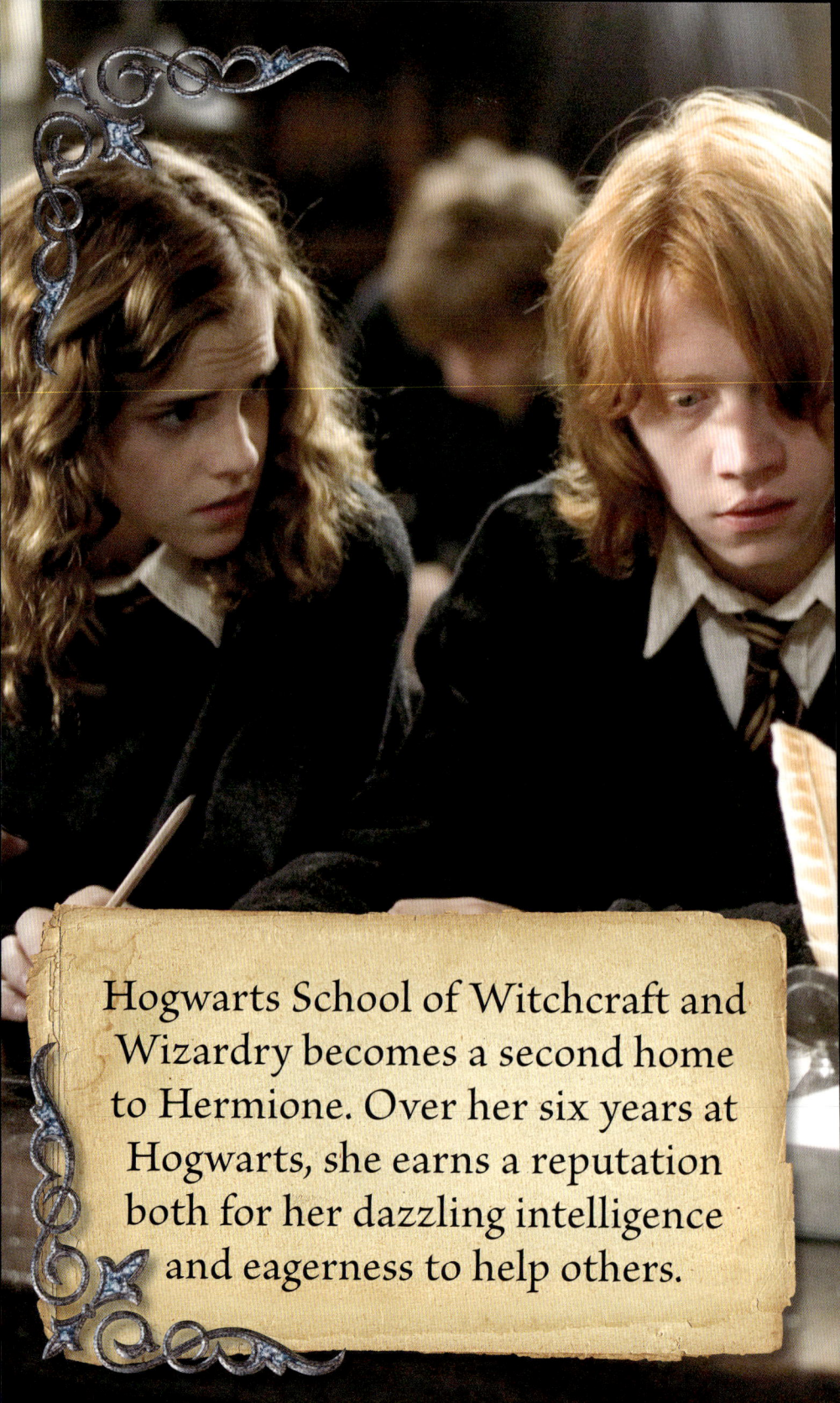

Hogwarts School of Witchcraft and Wizardry becomes a second home to Hermione. Over her six years at Hogwarts, she earns a reputation both for her dazzling intelligence and eagerness to help others.

Life at Hogwarts

After their arrival at Hogwarts, it's time to get sorted. Each student is placed into one of the four houses: Gryffindor, Hufflepuff, Ravenclaw or Slytherin.

Hermione is clever enough to be sorted into Ravenclaw, but, as she hoped, she's placed in Gryffindor.

Harry and Ron are also sorted into Gryffindor.

When they first meet, it doesn't seem as though Hermione, Harry and Ron will get along.

"Stop, stop, stop! You're going to take someone's eye out. Besides, you're saying it wrong. It's Levi*o*sa not Levio*sa*."

— HERMIONE GRANGER, HARRY POTTER AND THE PHILOSOPHER'S STONE film

A dangerous event forges the start of Hermione, Harry and Ron's extraordinary friendship.

Hermione is in the bathroom when a giant troll wanders in! Harry and Ron hear a troll is on the loose and go looking for Hermione to warn her.

Harry and Ron defeat the troll just in time. When the teachers appear and see that Harry and Ron have broken the rules by fighting the troll, Hermione takes the blame.

Hermione quickly proves herself to be a clever and dedicated student by excelling in all of her subjects.

"Do you take pride in being an insufferable know-it-all? Five points from Gryffindor!"

– Professor Snape to Hermione, Harry Potter and the Prisoner of Azkaban film

Hermione's teachers take notice of her intelligence and love of learning.

"Well, well, well, Hermione, you really are the brightest witch of your age I've ever met."

– PROFESSOR LUPIN,
HARRY POTTER AND THE PRISONER OF AZKABAN FILM

"They've yet to think of a spell that our Hermione can't do."

– RUBEUS HAGRID,
HARRY POTTER AND THE CHAMBER OF SECRETS FILM

But not all classes are easy for Hermione. In her third year, Hermione discovers the one Hogwarts subject she doesn't care for: Divination, the art of divining the future. Hermione prefers logical subjects without so much guesswork.

> "From the first moment you stepped foot in my class, I sensed that you did not possess the proper spirit for the noble art of Divination."
>
> – Professor Trelawney, *Harry Potter and the Prisoner of Azkaban* film

Hermione occasionally takes a break from her studies to have fun. She becomes the talk of Hogwarts when she attends the Yule Ball with famous Quidditch player Viktor Krum from Durmstrang.

Ron is jealous that Hermione goes to the Yule Ball with Viktor instead of with him.

"Next time there's a ball, pluck up the courage to ask me before somebody else does and not as a last resort!"

– Hermione Granger, *Harry Potter and the Goblet of Fire* film

Hermione starts off her time at Hogwarts as a stickler for the rules. However, as she gets older, she finds the value in breaking them occasionally.

"Now if you two don't mind, I'm going to bed before either of you come up with another clever idea to get us killed – or worse, expelled."

– HERMIONE GRANGER, *HARRY POTTER AND THE PHILOSOPHER'S STONE* FILM

> *"It's sort of exciting, isn't it? Breaking the rules."*
>
> — Hermione Granger, *Harry Potter and the Order of the Phoenix* film

Family, Friends and Foes

Hermione makes many friends in the wizarding world, including Harry, Ron and other fellow students. Hermione is a fierce and loyal friend who will stop at nothing to protect the people she cares about – even if that means putting herself in danger.

Hermione, just like Harry's mother, was born to Muggle parents.

Hermione comes from an ordinary and loving family.

Hermione: "My parents are dentists. They tend to people's teeth."

Professor Slughorn: "Fascinating, and is that considered a dangerous profession?"

– HARRY POTTER AND THE HALF-BLOOD PRINCE FILM

Hermione is often teased about having non-magical parents, especially by Draco Malfoy, who calls her a "Mudblood."

> "There are some wizards – like the Malfoy family – who think they're better than everyone else because they're what people call pureblood."
>
> – Rubeus Hagrid, *Harry Potter and the Chamber of Secrets* film

Draco and his friends.

Hermione's parents are proud she's a witch. However, she wipes their memories to keep them out of danger from Lord Voldemort's Death Eaters.

> "*Obliviate.*"
>
> – Hermione Granger,
> Harry Potter and the
> Deathly Hallows –
> Part 1 film

Hermione comforts her friends when they are upset.

In Defence Against the Dark Arts class, Mad-Eye Moody demonstrates the Cruciatus Curse, a torture spell that was used on Neville Longbottom's parents. After class, Hermione comforts Neville.

Hermione gives Harry a pep talk before he competes in the Triwizard Tournament.

Hermione: "The key is to concentrate. After that you just have to—"

Harry: "Battle a dragon."

– Harry Potter and the Goblet of Fire film

Hermione sticks by her friends' sides, even when there's danger.

In their sixth year, Hermione stays by Ron's hospital bedside after he accidentally drinks poison meant for Professor Dumbledore and ends up in the hospital wing.

When Hermione thinks that Sirius Black, an escapee from Azkaban prison, wants to hurt Harry, she puts herself in harm's way to protect him from danger.

"If you want to kill Harry, you'll have to kill us, too."

– HERMIONE GRANGER, *HARRY POTTER AND THE PRISONER OF AZKABAN* FILM

Hermione refuses to let Harry search for Lord Voldemort's hidden Horcruxes on his own. Hermione knows she needs to be by her friend's side on such a dangerous mission.

> "You don't really think you're going to be able to find all those Horcruxes by yourself, do you? You need us."
>
> – Hermione Granger, *Harry Potter and the Half-Blood Prince* film

Hermione refuses to divulge any secrets about their Horcrux hunt – even under torture by Bellatrix Lestrange, a vicious Death Eater.

Hermione is protective of the people she cares about most. She stands up for Hagrid and Buckbeak when Draco makes light of the Hippogriff's impending execution.

> *"You foul, loathsome, evil little cockroach!"*
>
> – Hermione Granger, *Harry Potter and the Prisoner of Azkaban* film

Cleverest Moments

Hermione is known at Hogwarts as the brightest witch of her age. On her many adventures with Harry and Ron, it is often thanks to Hermione's educated mind, grasp of logic and quick thinking that the trio safely escapes and succeeds.

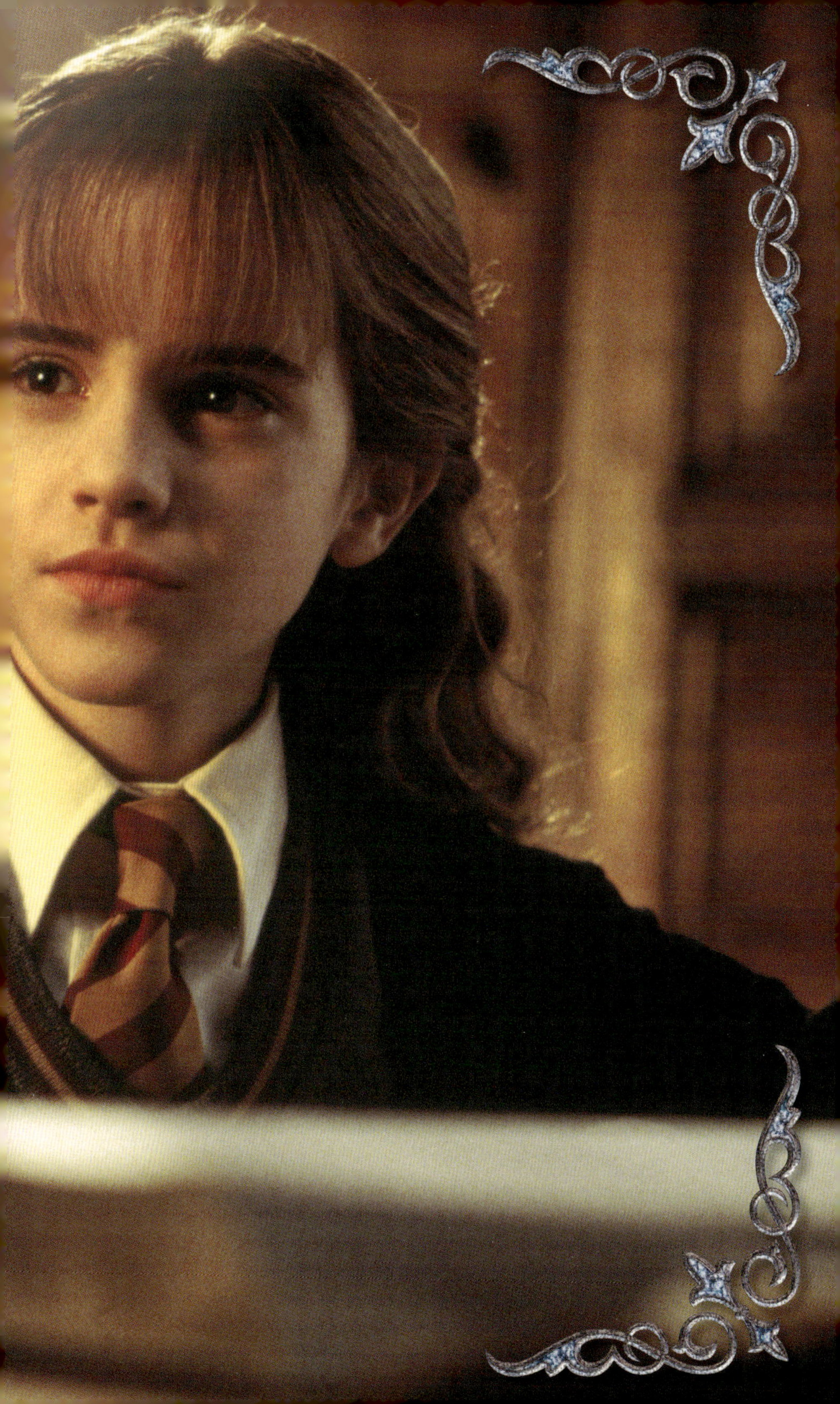

Hermione often saves the day by applying what she has learned in class to sticky situations.

Hermione is the one who realizes that Hagrid's three-headed dog, Fluffy, is standing on top of the trapdoor guarding the Philosopher's Stone.

Hermione uses her knowledge of Herbology, especially dangerous plants, to help Harry find the Philosopher's Stone hidden in Hogwarts castle.

"Devil's Snare, Devil's Snare... 'It's deadly fun... but will sulk in the sun!' That's it!"

– HERMIONE GRANGER, *HARRY POTTER AND THE PHILOSOPHER'S STONE* FILM

In their second year, Professor Lockhart frees a cage full of Cornish pixies in Defence Against the Dark Arts class.

Hermione is the only one who knows the spell that can stop the mischievous little creatures.

"Immobulus!"

– Hermione Granger, Harry Potter and the Chamber of Secrets film

Over the years, Hermione becomes an expert at brewing Polyjuice Potion, which allows the user to take on another person's appearance.

Hermione uses Polyjuice Potion to impersonate Death Eater Bellatrix Lestrange.

She also uses it to sneak into the Ministry of Magic with Harry and Ron.

Through research at the library, Hermione discovers that the mysterious beast in the Chamber of Secrets is a Basilisk, also known as the King of Serpents.

Anyone who looks a Basilisk *directly* in the eye will perish.

Hermione sees the Basilisk *indirectly* in a mirror. She survives, but is Petrified – literally turned to stone.

Before being Petrified, Hermione left a clue about the Basilisk for Harry and Ron to find.

Thanks to Hermione, Harry is able to defeat the Basilisk and save Hogwarts from its terror and destruction.

Hermione uses a Time-Turner to go back in time to save Hagrid's Hippogriff, Buckbeak, and Harry's godfather, Sirius Black.

Hermione and Harry watch as past events unfold.

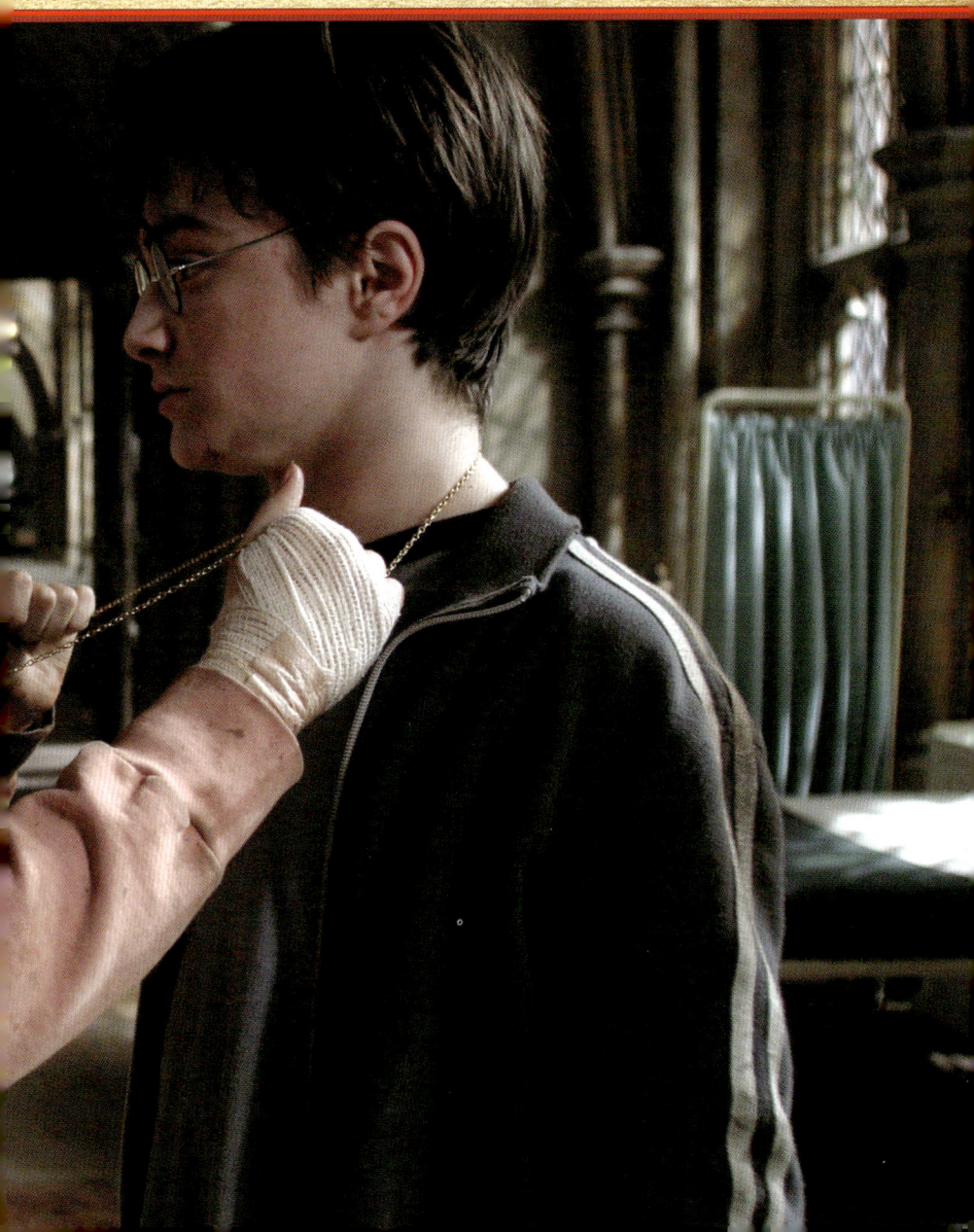

While on the run with Harry and Ron, Hermione puts an Undetectable Extension Charm on her small, purple bag. That way Hermione can be prepared for any situation.

The charm allows the inside of the bag to expand to fit whatever she needs to carry, while appearing to be its original size on the outside.

She keeps a magical tent in the bag that comes in very handy while they are hunting for Horcruxes.

When Ron gets Splinched after Disapparating from the Ministry, Hermione uses the Essence of Dittany she keeps in her bag to heal his wounds.

When Harry, Ron and Hermione break into Gringotts in disguise to find a Horcrux, their cover is blown and Hermione must find a way to get them out alive.

Hermione: "Who's got an idea?"

Ron: "You're the brilliant one."

Hermione: "I've got something, but it's mad!"

– Harry Potter and the
Deathly Hallows – Part 2 film

Hermione daringly jumps onto the fire-breathing dragon that guards the Gringotts vaults. It bursts through the roof, soaring through the sky with Hermione, Ron and Harry holding on for their lives.

Fighting Dark Forces

Hermione's determination and pluck, combined with her brilliance at spells, make her one of Harry Potter's strongest allies. She fights by his side at a number of important battles.

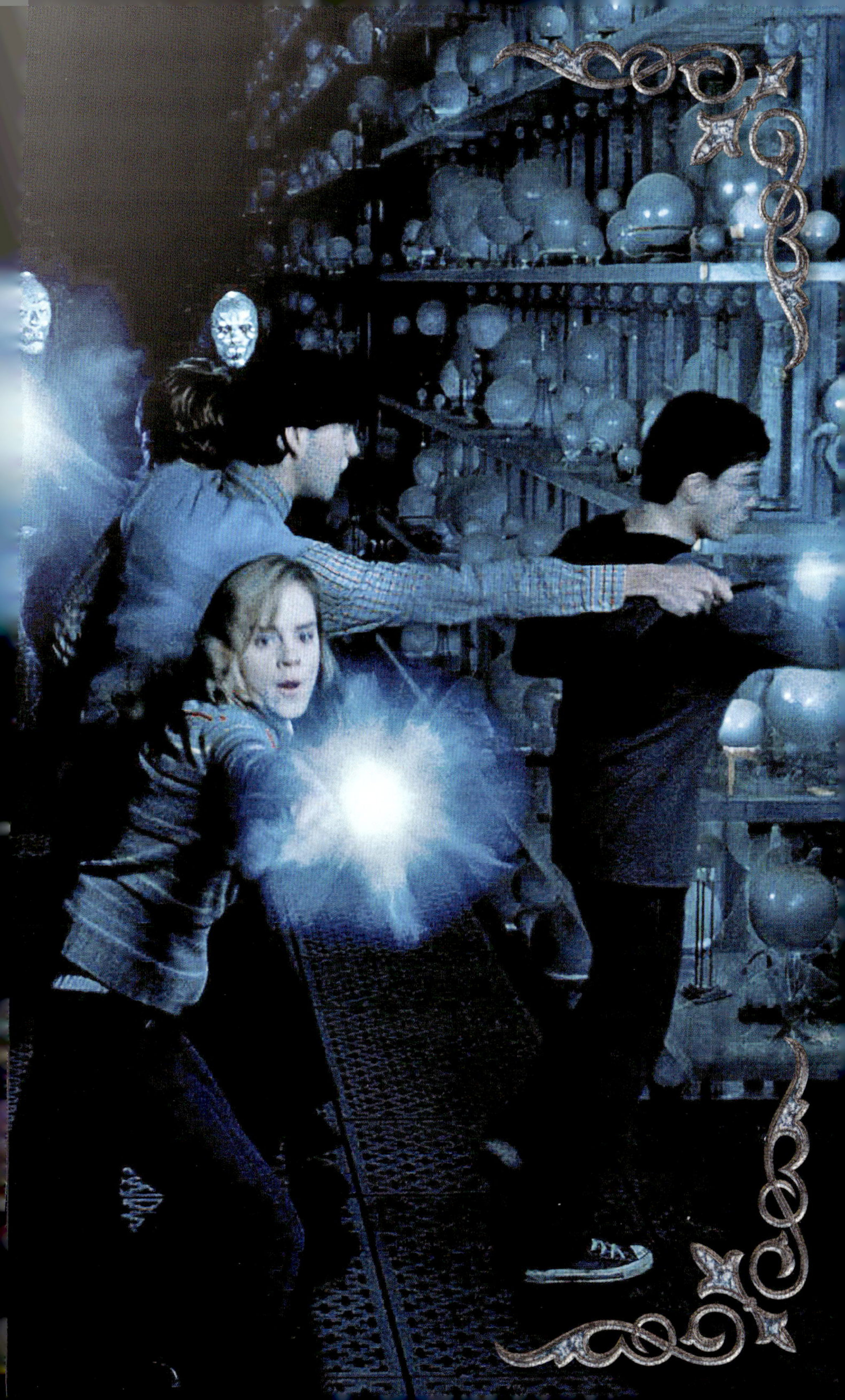

In her fifth year, Hermione has the idea to start the secret group Dumbledore's Army to teach her fellow students how to defend themselves against Dark magic.

Hermione convinces Harry to teach their classmates defensive magic.

"We've got to be able to defend ourselves. And if Umbridge refuses to teach us how, we need someone who will."

— HERMIONE GRANGER, *HARRY POTTER AND THE ORDER OF THE PHOENIX* film

During a DA session, students learn to produce a Patronus, a spell that wards off Dementors.

Members of Dumbledore's Army have their skills put to the test.

When a group of Snatchers discovers Hermione, Harry and Ron's hiding place in the woods, Hermione thinks fast and figures out a way to buy them time to disguise who they truly are.

Hermione uses a spell to make Harry's face swell, making it difficult for the Snatchers to recognize him.

The Snatchers take them to Malfoy Manor in the hope that Draco will be able to identify his former classmates.

Hermione plays a crucial part in the final battle of Hogwarts and Lord Voldemort's ultimate downfall.

Hermione and Ron go into the Chamber of Secrets in search of a Basilisk fang that will destroy the lost diadem of Ravenclaw, a Horcrux.

Hermione and Ron are so relieved to be alive they finally admit their true feelings for each other and kiss.

"We wouldn't last two days without her."

– Ron Weasley, Harry Potter and the Deathly Hallows – Part 2 film